TABLE OF CONTENTS

Unless otherwise indicated, all Scripture quotations are taken from the King James Version of the Bible.
The Uncommon Minister - A 52-Week Protégé Program For Those Called Into Ministry
ISBN 1-56394-319-0/B-241
Copyright © 2006 by **MIKE MURDOCK**
All publishing rights belong exclusively to Wisdom International
Publisher/Editor: Deborah Murdock Johnson
Published by The Wisdom Center · 4051 Denton Hwy. · Ft. Worth, Texas 76117
1-817-759-BOOK · 817-759-0300
You Will Love Our Website...! WisdomOnline.com

Accuracy Department: To our Friends and Partners...We welcome any comments on errors or misprints you find in our book...Email our department: AccuracyDept@thewisdomcenter.tv. Your aid in helping us excel is highly valued.

Anything You Do Not Have
Is Stored In Someone
Near You And Love Is
The Secret Map
To The Treasure.

-MIKE MURDOCK

WHY I WROTE THIS BOOK

I Love Preachers.

Everywhere I travel, I find ministers who are troubled, angry, sad and disappointed with their own progress in their ministry. Unreasonable goals, the trap of *comparison* with other ministries, mental exhaustion from trying to understand damaged congregations has often left us disillusioned about our own success for God. Yes, we are masters at disguising our disappointments, justifying unreached goals, and yet finding it impossible to get away from the ever present flame of hope within us...that God's potential could be unleashed at any time.

I was born into the ministry. My father pastored for fifty-seven years. We had two family altars each day—morning and night. My mother insisted on the memorization of a Scripture every day of my life. I preached my first sermon at the age of 8 in Waco, Texas, under my father's ministry. Later, at the age of nine, he permitted me to speak with him at various tent crusades. At the age of 15, friends of my father opened their doors for ministry to their congregations and youth groups. I attended Bible college for three semesters, then on February 9, 1966, I began my first evangelistic crusade as a young evangelist. That was over 40 years ago. After 40 countries and over 16,000 audiences, many Keys, Laws and Wisdom Principles have become evident. Sitting at the supper table with the most Uncommon Ministers of my generation has unlocked many secrets—secrets that created "The Uncommon Minister."

Preachers are not alike.

Ministers are as different from each other as lawyers, fathers and salesmen.

Personalities differ. Goals are different. Their training is different. Their knowledge levels are different. Their pain is even different.

Doctors often cooperate for a mutual cause.

Lawyers often cooperate for a single benefit.

Farmers will link tractors to send a message to America.

Yet, ministers rarely cooperate together for a common cause.

Doctors are thrilled over the discoveries of another doctor. Actors will even hold annual celebration events to express recognition of the uniqueness of each.

Meanwhile, ministers of the Gospel often challenge, argue, stain and even publicly sneer at the discoveries, revelations or goals of another.

Still, the Heavenly Father Who has *called* us, *anointed* us and *empowered* us to heal our broken generation insists we "love one another." Jesus said it clearly. "A new commandment I give unto you, That ye love one another; as I have loved you, that ye also love one another. By this shall all men know that ye are My disciples, if ye have love one to another," (John 13:34-35).

Anything You Do Not Have Is Stored In Someone Near You, And Love Is The Secret Map To The Treasure.

Your ministry can become *satisfying* to you.

Your ministry can *multiply* in its effectiveness.

Your ministry can become a *healing power.*

Your ministry can become *greater* than ever.

Your ministry can *increase in joy.*

The Key? The Wisdom of God.

That is why I wrote this book.

Mike Murdock

My Personal Prayer For Your Ministry

"Holy Spirit, use these simple words to unlock the greatness in the leaders You have chosen and anointed for my generation. Stir up the gift within us. Place Your coals of fire on our tongues, purify our words and strengthen our determination to walk in absolute obedience. Awaken a new passion for Your Word. Reveal steps that will unleash the waves of Wisdom for our people. Use us as Trophies of Divine Greatness to display what You can do with anyone who hears Your voice and obeys. In the name of Jesus, I pray. Amen."

━━━━━━━►▷·◦·◁◄━━━━━━━

"The Spirit of the Lord is upon me, because He hath anointed me to preach the gospel to the poor; He hath sent me to heal the brokenhearted, to preach deliverance to the captives, and recovering of sight to the blind, to set at liberty them that are bruised, To preach the acceptable year of the Lord," (Luke 4:18-19).

The Word Of God
Becomes
The Energy Of God
Within You.

-MIKE MURDOCK

❧ 1 ❧

KNOW YOUR BIBLE FOR YOURSELF

The Word Of God Is Your Life.

The Word of God is the greatest Book on earth.

It is the *revelation* of God. It is Truth. It is Holy. It is powerful. It heals. It energizes. It corrects. It changes YOU.

The Word is the only Force that changes *those who hear you.*

When I was about 23 or 24 years old, I accepted an invitation for a crusade in Texas. The pastor had built one of the strongest churches ever in Houston, Texas.

Late one night, I ventured a question. "Would you critique and analyze my ministry for me? I respect you and truly want you to tell me what I am doing wrong or how I could improve my ministry." (Actually, I wanted him to affirm me and tell me all the things he liked about my ministry, but he did not do that. He responded to the question I had asked him.)

"Mike, in my early years, I had a ministry much like your own. Then, I went to England. The people patiently listened for a few months. Then, they began to approach me and tell me they appreciated my stories and illustrations, but they really had a desire to simply hear what The Word of God said about their problems and the solutions it offered."

He continued, "It hurt me deeply, but when I went to prayer, God began to show me how to help the people become *dependent* upon The Word of God for their answers and solutions. Parables and stories were to confirm and reveal how The Word of God could be applied. Yet, they never got tired of hearing The Word of God and specific Scriptures that applied to their lives."

He implied that my messages contained very few Scriptures. He was correct. I cringed. It hurt. I was devastated emotionally. However, I was honest with myself and agreed that my messages were really two or three arguments and illustrations instead of the actual Word of God.

The Uncommon Minister must develop an obsession for *understanding the mind of God.*

You see, the mind of God is revealed through The Word of God. His opinion of sin is revealed in The Word. His opinion of homosexuality is revealed in The Word. His opinion of *prosperity* is revealed in The Word. His guidelines for a *productive life* are revealed in The Word.

5 Helpful Keys Every Minister Should Remember

1. **Your Bible Is Your Wisdom Book, Not Your Sermon Book.** Many preachers only read the Scriptures while searching for a sermon for their people. The Word of God is not a part of their personal life.

2. **Read The Word Daily.** *Habit Will Take You Further Than Desire.* Habitual exposure to the heart of God will create incredible results.

When you read the biographies of uncommon spiritual leaders such as Smith Wigglesworth and others—they had a *daily obsession* for The Word of God. It quickened and energized them. It lifted their spirits during times of oppression. It kept them *focused.* It *fueled* their hatred of sin and unleashed an *uncommon faith* in their own goals and Assignment.

3. **Personalize Your Bible By Marking Scriptures Impressing You.** My Bible has a distinct marking system. It has changed this year. I highlight in *pink* every Scripture that I have memorized. ("Thy Word have I hid in mine heart.") *Blue* marking is used for any truth concerning The Holy Spirit or The Word of God. *Green* marking concerns finances or blessings. *Yellow* underlining occurs when a Scripture is worthy of reviewing, memorizing or using in a specific study.

4. **Customize Your Bible With Pictures Or Important Notes.** Tape important information on the blank pages in your Bible. A long-time friend, opened his Bible one day to me. He had taped poems, biographical comments and powerful outlines from others

throughout his Bible. His Bible was one of the most intriguing, fascinating and delightful books I had ever seen. It *excited* me. *Personalize* your Bible as your personal Success Handbook any way that you desire.

5. **Establish A Daily System For Reading Your Bible.** Several exist. Many years ago, I would read a small book (James or Titus) over and over again. Within a month, I would read the book of James 40 or 50 times. Imagine the incredible truths that began to leap off the pages! What you keep reading continually, you understand more completely.

Topical Study is selecting a particular topic and exhausting your research on it. Each morning for 30 days, I have taken a subject such as healing, the blood of Christ or prosperity and marked every Scripture relating to it. It deepens your knowledge and enables you to even become an authority on that topic within a few months.

Reading the Bible *chronologically,* Genesis through Revelation, is the most common way of reading The Scriptures. Three chapters a day and five on Sunday enable you to read the Bible through once a year. For many years, I have read 40 chapters a day. This enables me to complete the Bible every 30 days. It provides an overview that is remarkable.

Whatever you do, *establish a system.* Change it when you desire. However, always have a system for reading The Word.

Know Your Bible For Yourself.

It is One of the Secrets of the Uncommon Minister.

RECOMMENDED INVESTMENTS:
My Wisdom Journal (Book/B-163/160 Pages/$20)
31 Scriptures Every Minister Should Memorize (Book/B-201/32 Pages/$3)
The Minister's Topical Bible (Book/B-217/400 Pages/$10)
The Uncommon Minister, Series 1 (6 Tapes/TS-46/$30)
The Uncommon Minister, Series 2 (6 Tapes/TS-47/$30)

Recognition Of Your Worth
Creates Confidence;
Recognition Of Your Lack
Creates Humility.

-MIKE MURDOCK

❧ 2 ❧

ENCOURAGE YOUR PEOPLE TO IDENTIFY AND PURSUE THEIR OWN DISTINCT ASSIGNMENT

Every Person Was Created For A Purpose.

Your people were created to become *Problem-Solvers.* The problem they were created to solve is their *Assignment.* Dentists solve teeth problems. Lawyers solve legal problems. Mothers solve emotional problems.

Meditate on your people. Do you know the problems they were created to solve? Many pastors do not even know the jobs, careers or passions of their congregation. Sometimes, our messages do not quite relate to the specific goals and dreams of those we love and serve.

I flew to a crusade and was picked up by a very interesting young man, representing his pastor and church. As we drove to the hotel, he shared with me his dream. He longed to start his own business. The front seat was filled with books relating to his goals and dreams. He was very excited. He had been meeting with different mentors regarding this Assignment. I listened carefully. I asked numerous questions and that excited him. As he shared his goal, his face glowed. His conversation was animated and filled with genuine enthusiasm. He was building his whole life around his dream, that Assignment he felt so strong within him.

When I discussed this with his pastor the next day, the pastor seemed genuinely surprised.

"I have never really known quite what his business was about," the pastor confessed. "But, he has been attending our church for some time."

Several years ago, an elder in a church where I had ministered died. When she died, the pastor did not even know her address. He had never even shared a meal with her personally, though *she had been on the staff for almost ten years.*

He used her *gifts.*

He trusted her *judgment.*

He received her *offerings.*

Yet, he was uninterested in her own personal goals and dreams. This is tragic.

God did not create the *people* for the ministry.

God created the *ministry* for the people.

Your people need you...Your caring.

Your people need your counsel concerning their Assignment, their goals and dreams. Move toward them. Secure their business cards and keep them in your Personal Prayer Book in your Secret Place.

5 Helpful Keys In Making Your Ministry More Effective In The Every Day Life And Routine Of Your People

1. **Remind Yourself Daily That Your Own Assignment As A Minister Is To Connect Your People To Their Assignment On The Earth.**

2. **Have Your People Complete A "Dreams And Goals Sheet."** Keep it in notebooks in your Secret Place of prayer. Pray over those dreams and goals.

3. **Request A Business Card Or Photograph Of Their Personal Business Or Place Where They Work Each Day.** Keep that for times of intercession.

4. **Talk To Your People With A Genuine Desire To Understand Them In Light Of Their Home And Focus.** You see, their world is not the Church. Their world is not preparing sermons for others. They face rejection, anger, temptation and hundreds of situations *without* a strong knowledge of The Word.

5. **Interrogate Them Continuously About Their Progress Towards Their Goals And Assignment.** Jesus did. Simon Peter went fishing. He caught nothing. When the morning was come, Jesus calls out, "Children, have ye any meat?" (John 21:5). Jesus continuously showed an interest in *their* pain, *their* victories and *their* progress. Their pain was *His door* into their lives.

When you understand the needs, fears and goals of your people, your instructions to them can become more relevant, useable, pursued and celebrated.

Jesus Noted The Jobs Of Those He Loved. When the disciples expressed their loss to Jesus, He said simply, "Cast the net on the right side of the ship, and ye shall find," (John 21:6). You, too, can have this same impact.

Happy Sheep should be the obsession of the *Uncommon Shepherd.* That is why the Great Shepherd instructed, "Feed My sheep," (see John 21:15-17).

Encourage Your People To Identify And Pursue Their Own Unique Assignment.

It is One of the Secrets of the Uncommon Minister.

Give Another What
He Cannot Find
Anywhere Else
And He Will
Keep Returning.

-MIKE MURDOCK

❧ 3 ❧

DO NOT OVERLOOK THE WOUNDED NEAREST YOU

Focus Often Blinds You.

It is the "downside" of focus. It is the negative side of obsession for your calling. As a minister, you have goals and dreams. You become obsessed and focused. Your daily agenda revolves around that obsession. Every conversation contributes to that dream you are attempting to birth. You are fighting, clawing and exhausting every ounce of your being...to complete your Assignment on earth.

Yet, somebody near you is *hurting. Can you feel it?* Is your family withdrawing? They may become introspective. Many times, they become reluctant to speak up. They see your stress, burdens and busyness. They feel unimportant, insignificant and unnecessary.

They believe any pursuit of your attention is considered an interruption or distraction. They feel it. They know it.

Study Your Inner Circle. Your *real ministry* begins with those nearest you. That is why Jesus took His disciples aside, away from the multitude. "And the apostles gathered themselves together unto Jesus, and told Him all things, both what they had done, and what they had taught. And He said unto them, Come ye yourselves apart into a desert place, and rest a while: for there were many coming and going, and they had no leisure so much as to eat," (Mark 6:30-31).

4 Things You Should Know About Those Nearest You

1. **Those Who Minister For You Will Often Require Ministry From You.** Last night, this occurred to me. Three of us were working in my Wisdom Room on a project. I was consumed with a book. I had fought hard to preserve this private time, away from the pulpit and traveling. Suddenly, one of my staff began to cry. It

dawned on me immediately that she had asked me several hours earlier to pray for her father. He was in a dangerous and critical condition in the hospital a thousand miles away. I had *intended* to pray for him, but my book was my obsession. As she sat there, her mind could not disconnect from the love she had for her father.

I was wrong. I had overlooked the needs of someone nearest me. I immediately stopped, apologized and called a special time of prayer.

2. **Someone Who Never Causes Trouble Is Usually Ignored.** This occurred to me some months ago. My general manager mentioned a very difficult situation one of the staff members was facing. I was stunned. They had been living with this problem for a long time. I had not known it. Why? She was not a complainer, nor a whiner. She was a thankful person.

She was *not* a reacher.

She was *not* a manipulator, maneuvering everyone toward the solution of her problem.

She was quiet, shy and *alone.* Others who had experienced similar problems were often demanding, vocal and outspoken. So they received the attention they wanted.

Quiet children need attention even more than *opinionated children.* Yet, they are often overlooked.

3. **Your Most Supportive People Will Seldom Reveal Their Deepest Needs And Wounds.** While praying recently, The Holy Spirit reminded me of one of the staff members. "When did they receive their last raise?" I asked my general manager.

"I do not really know," was her reply, "but I will find out."

She had not received a raise in over two years of working for the ministry. She had never complained. She had never griped. Yet, I had overlooked her needs.

My mail often piles up. Phone calls pour in by the hundreds to my office every week. Everyone seems to be in crisis.

Are you only responding to the loudest?

Are you only responding to the most obnoxious?

Are you only responding to the most persistent?

That is why the families of ministers are often the last to receive our attention. Our staff is too often the last to receive our favor.

4. **Those Nearest Us Should Be The First To Receive The Fruit Of Our Love, Blessings And Attention.** Who needs a special season of *restoration* and relaxation? Who needs a *listening*

ear? Who is being ignored by others? Who is in a true financial crisis? "Withhold not good from them to whom it is due, when it is in the power of thine hand to do it," (Proverbs 3:27).

Do Not Overlook The Wounded Nearest You.

It is One of the Secrets of the Uncommon Minister.

Your Goals Decide
The Value You Place
On Your Time.

-MIKE MURDOCK

∽ 4 ∽

CONTINUALLY REVIEW AND UPDATE YOUR MINISTRY GOALS

Your Ministry Goals Will Change.
Continuously.

Someday, you will look back at this very moment and be amazed at the goals you presently have. Things so vital to you at 20 years old will become unimportant to you at 30.

When I was beginning my ministry, I wanted very much to minister in many different states and cities. For some reason, it made me feel successful, desired and accepted when I received invitations from many *different* places. Today, *staying home* excites me! Knowing that my books are being read in many places is more satisfying to me than traveling.

The greatest goal of my life today is staying in my Secret Place of prayer and writing what The Holy Spirit teaches me.

I remember well the excitement over hiring my first secretary. At last, someone would help me do all the typing! Today, over 60 associates here at my offices work diligently around the clock producing and processing mail, books, tapes and videos. *Times* have changed. *Needs* have changed. My *personal goals* have changed.

It will happen to you, too.

Your present feelings are not permanent. Your present opinions are probably temporary. Your present views have been sculptured by your past experiences. *New experiences* are coming. *New relationships* are ahead. Stay conscious of this.

Never Make Permanent Decisions Because Of Temporary Feelings.

15 Keys Concerning Your Dreams
And Goals

1. **Recognize That Others Cannot Discern What Is Important To You At This Point.** You alone can decide what generates your joy. Have you ever been agitated when someone became too aggressive or pushy in trying to get you to bowl, play tennis or golf when you knew those things did not excite you? You see, people want you to enjoy what *they* like!

Few friends will ever understand your unique tastes, desires and excitements. Some love parties while others prefer a prayer meeting. Some love shopping, others love studying.

2. **Discern And Treasure Anything Or Anyone That Energizes And Motivates You.** Reading, motorcycles, travel, learning another language, working in your flower garden, painting, shopping or playing golf. Name it to yourself. Know what you love. *Know what you truly enjoy.* You see, few people really do know the things that they enjoy. They *watch* life instead of *living* life. Millions stare at a television set day after day without having any idea of the life they could live personally. They are watching *others* live the life they covet.

3. **Stop Apologizing To Those Who Do Not Understand What You Love.** I have an insatiable desire to learn. Reading excites me. Something drives me to write books. When I complete a book, I feel exhilarated. Thrilled. Excited. I feel progress when I dictate a significant portion of a book.

Learning is ecstasy to me.

Many friends do not grasp this sensitivity within me. They urge me to "play golf." I do not understand golfers. While many of my friends enjoy hitting a small ball hundreds of yards, then hitting it further and further for hours—it baffles me. I do not understand the fascination of golfing.

They do not understand my fascination with learning! So when they drop by my office, they always want to preach me a little sermon on the importance of "relaxing." *Their discussion on relaxation is more stressful than anything else I am doing!* While I am listening to their boring and uninteresting lecture on "taking time off," I could be generating incredible joy and progress through dictation on a book. They are attempting to be helpful. Actually, I consider them a distraction!

4. Do Not Depend On Others To Understand Your Dreams And Goals. Permit them *their* individuality. They have every right to love the things they love. However, refuse to be intimidated by their efforts to persuade you to adopt their lifestyle.

5. Accept That Many May Not Celebrate What You Are Pursuing. They do not treasure those things that are important to you. This can be heartbreaking when those you love seem disinterested.

6. Determine What Matters To You More Than Anything Else. Your spiritual goals must become the *most* important goals. Your financial dreams require attention. Your physical goals deserve attention as well.

7. Invest One Hour In Writing Down Clearly The Things That Really Matter To You At This Point Of Your Ministry. You can keep it confidential, private and away from prying eyes. You must *continuously* assess and evaluate any *changing* of goals you are experiencing in your ministry.

8. Permit Unexciting Dreams Of Yesterday To Die. Stop pursuing something that does not have the ability to excite you anymore. Do not feel obligated to keep attempting to obtain it...if you are now in a different place in your life. Perhaps, you wanted to own a motorcycle ten years ago. You never bought one. Now, you have the money to purchase it, but the excitement over it has died. Do not buy it now! That season has passed. Permit it to die.

9. Do Not Expect Everyone On Your Staff To Always Pursue Great Dreams For Themselves. You cannot *force* them. *Encourage* them. However, you cannot *force* greatness on anyone.

Several years ago, I became excited about helping some of my staff achieve maximum physical fitness. Purchasing a special building, I filled it with the best workout equipment available. Then, I hired a special trainer ($75 an hour) to give personal attention and teaching. Within three weeks, only two showed up. Each had their own excuse for not working out. It was across the street from the office. It did not cost anyone a cent. Yet, I could not force it on them.

I have a beautiful gym at my home. It contains a wonderful basketball court, workout areas, and is ideal for a top physical fitness program. Yet, the friends closest to me continually give excuses when I ask them to come work out with me. The *only* person encouraging me is my trainer! Occasionally, I hold a self-pity party for myself. Sometimes, I feel somewhat alone in my huge gym. Even so, it keeps me reminded that you cannot force others to grow their own Seeds of Greatness.

Success is an individual decision. Nobody else can make it for you. You cannot make it for anyone else either.

You may become discouraged from being the only person in your family making a maximum effort. Working out alone is not fun. However, let me encourage you to grow the picture of your dream bigger...bigger and bigger. Do not quit. Determine to experience your dream whether anyone else around you experiences it or not.

10. Understand That Others May Need To See You Succeed First. Many become demoralized and discouraged with themselves. They want to see you succeed *before* they make any attempts again. As you give yourself to your goals, something can catch fire within them.

11. Avoid Intimate Relationships With Those Who Do Not Really Respect Your Dreams. You will have to sever ties. *Wrong people do not always leave your life voluntarily.*

I have experienced friends sitting in my gym, laughing at me trying to develop myself. They have attempted to "talk me out of body building." You do not need anyone close to you raining on your parade. Life is too short to permit discouragers close to you.

12. Place Photographs Of Your Desired Future On The Walls Around You. "Write the vision, make it plain upon tables, that he may run that readeth it," (Habakkuk 2:2). *Write* your dreams. Put pictures around you. *They motivate you.* Wisdom Key #2: *When Your Heart Decides The Destination, Your Mind Will Design The Map To Reach It.*

13. You Must Learn The Secret Of Encouraging Yourself In Your Ministry. Avoid the presence of cynics, critics and fault-finders. Your own family may find reasons you should quit, lower your goals and try something easier. Do not fall for it. *Stay focused.* Wisdom Key #229: *What You Hear Determines What You Feel.*

14. Choose Your Friends Instead Of Letting Your Friends Choose You.

Who Are The Seven People Who Create Energy In Your Presence?

Who Are The Seven Most Respectful Protégés Under Your

Mentorship?

Who Are The Seven Most Trustworthy People In Your Life?

15. Identify Those Who Have Become Burdens Instead Of Burden-Bearers. Some enter your life with a "desire to help." Within weeks, they have become burdens instead. Analyze and evaluate on a consistent basis those who have become difficult, obnoxious and troublesome. Then identify those who really lift the burdens from your life. Celebrate them. Provide access. Avoid permitting them to overwork themselves. Good people can become burdensome to us if we do not protect them as well.

When you assess and evaluate your goals, you will unclutter your life of the unnecessary.

Continually Review And Update Your Ministry Goals.

It is One of the Secrets of the Uncommon Minister.

When God Wants
To Bless You,
He Brings A Person
Into Your Life.

-MIKE MURDOCK

～ 5 ～

TREASURE YOUR MINISTRY MAILING LIST

Friendships Are Golden Gifts From God.
Partners of your ministry are invaluable.

When I was 18 years old, I spoke in a small country church in Louisiana. At the close of the service, the pastor approached me.

"I noticed you are selling your records. My son takes the name and address of every person who purchases his album. So, when he produces a new album, his previous customers always purchase his new one immediately. Son, you ought to start collecting the names of every person who hears you minister."

Well, I was 18...An *ignorant* eighteen. I did not want to take the time to do it. So, I did not do it...until I was almost 30 years old. That is when I started seriously considering documenting the names of every person who had sat under my ministry. That pastor's son? He ended up selling millions and millions of records and tapes throughout the world. He became one of the most famous names throughout Christianity.

He knew the importance of a name.

Three men flew from Phoenix, Arizona, to my home in Houston, Texas, when I was about 30 years old. They had analyzed my ministry. They declared that I was "destined for significance" and wanted to participate in my growing ministry. They had quite a resume. Two of the most powerful ministries in the United States had hired them in previous years. They questioned me about my "mailing list." Well, I really did not have a serious mailing list. When someone wrote me, I answered. However, I did not keep constant and regular contact with them.

"How many monthly partners do you have in your ministry?" They asked.

I confessed that I did not have *any* monthly partners. Explaining that I was a *church* evangelist, I told them that most pastors did not want the names of their people given to evangelists. In fact, one major pastor had complimented me saying, "I really appreciate that you never ask for financial help for your ministry. If you did, I would not allow you to place your newsletter on the table in my church. I do not want my people writing other ministries."

As I explained this to them, they asked another penetrating question.

"Do you have *enough finances* to do *everything* God has told you to do with your ministry?"

"Of course not," I replied. "I do not even have enough money to hire a secretary or rent an office. My present office is in my garage."

"Then, how will you ever be able to complete your instructions from God *without partners* to help you financially?"

It angered me. They were correct, of course. Yet, I had taken *great pride in the fact that I never asked for financial help.* Pastors had even expressed their appreciation of this. No, I did not have one single monthly partner. I simply traveled night after night, week after week, year after year pouring my life out. Whatever was given to me as an offering, I lived on. Yet, I did not have enough money to publish books, make cassette tapes or even purchase a home. The offerings were simply enough to buy gasoline, a car and keep traveling day after day.

These consultants told me bluntly and boldly that my ministry would never succeed significantly *until I valued the names of those who cared*...potential partners who could help me spread this Gospel. I became belligerent, and invited them to leave my home.

Some months later, I sat at my desk with work overwhelming me. I desperately needed a secretary. My garage was crammed full of boxes. That moment, I realized I had to overcome my pride, *write my closest friends and ask for their *monthly* support.

That was the beginning of explosive growth.

A number of my friends wrote back and agreed to assist me. A secretary was hired. My first office was established. The songs, the books and the teaching tapes began to roll through me...because I truly *valued* those God had brought into my life and ministry.

Today, my ministry partners are more important to me than words can convey. Golden Gifts From God.

3 Things You Should Know About The Importance Of A Name

1.   **Every Successful Pastor Knows The Importance Of A Name.** That is why visitor cards are given out each service. Receptions where greeters meet newcomers are held every Sunday morning. Millions of dollars are spent on television programs, radio broadcasts and newspaper ads, because *people* are important to your vision.

2.   **Every Successful Businessman Knows The Importance Of A Single Name.** Listen to Ron Popeil, a multimillionaire who has succeeded greatly. "One of the mandates at Ronco, beside quality and innovation, is this: A name, address and phone number are worth gold. We always capture a telephone number in addition to the name and address of a customer, because those items are very common, very valuable." (Page 219, *The Salesman of the Century.*)

3.   **Friendships Are Too Precious To Lose.** They cost too much to treat lightly. I read once where former President George Bush had 7,500 names on his Rolodex files. He loves people. He values people. He knows *the importance of a name.*

Treasure Your Ministry Mailing List.

It is One of the Secrets of the Uncommon Minister.

RECOMMENDED INVESTMENTS:
Seeds of Wisdom on Relationships (Book/B-14/32 Pages/$3)
The Double Diamond Principle in Successful Relationships (6 Tapes/TS-16/ $30)

Mentorship Is Wisdom Without The Pain.

-MIKE MURDOCK

～ 6 ～

KEEP YOUR IPOD FULL OF MENTORSHIP TEACHINGS AND WORDS FROM UNCOMMON ACHIEVERS

You Must Receive Before You Give.

Last night, I flew in from a crusade in Houston. I arrived at 9:30 p.m., but had to remain on the runway for a long time due to early arrival. It was midnight when I finally arrived home. Though tired, I ran my bath water and relaxed. The day had been a full one. I did not feel like reading, cleaning up my house or anything else. Yet, I knew the power of simply *listening.* So, I played a cassette tape of one of the most effective business writers in America. He was conducting an interview with a major motivational speaker. It was tremendous. Though I was too fatigued to study, my time for bathing and getting ready for bed was not wasted. The tape was still playing when I drifted off to sleep an hour later. Wisdom Key #106: *Mentorship Is Wisdom Without The Pain.*

Mentorship can take place any moment of the day when you plan ahead for such opportunities.

While getting dressed or cleaning your room, you can listen to your ipod.

If you eat lunch alone, this is an ideal time to receive special teaching from someone, listening to your ipod.

Mentorship is so important. Mentors are those who know something you do not know. They have been where you want to go. They have accomplished something significant that you admire. Most Uncommon Achievers care deeply about others and long to impart their secrets to them.

Do not lose these moments.

7 Keys Every Minister Should Know About Personal Mentorship

1. **Listen To Your Mentorship Talk More Than Once.** I discovered early that I rarely heard everything on a tape when I listened the first time. Listening several times revealed that I had missed important information on the first or second listening.

2. **When You Hear Something Vital And Essential, Stop And Play It Back Again Immediately.** When you keep listening to it, it will get inside your spirit and heart. Wisdom Key #29: *What You Repeatedly Hear, You Eventually Believe.*

3. **Write, In A Special Notebook, Those Things You Want To Remember From Your Ipod Listening.**

4. **Stop And Picture The Truth That Is Taking Place.** Visualization is a powerful way to *keep something that you are hearing.* (See Habakkuk 2:2.)

5. **Talk To Other Ministers About The Secret You Learned.** Discuss it and how it can apply to their ministry.

6. **Keep Your Ipod Visible And Accessible At All Times.** Take advantage of every spare moment.

7. **Listen To A Variety Of Mentors.** Do not limit yourself to one school of thought. Listen to businessmen. Listen to motivational speakers. Listen to cassette tapes of missionaries, pastors and evangelists. Every person has been given a different view and has experienced a variation of events in their lives.

Learn from many. The Holy Spirit used 40 different authors over a 1,600 year period to document the Scriptures. Each author was inspired to focus on something different...*for a reason.*

Keep Your Ipod Full Of Mentorship Teachings And Words From Uncommon Achievers.

It is One of the Secrets of the Uncommon Minister.

⟋ 7 ⟍

GIVE ATTENTION TO THE OFFERINGS OF YOUR PEOPLE

Offerings Matter To God.

Offerings matter to people.

Offerings *should* matter to *you*.

It is the Uncommon Minister of the Gospel who *willingly* unlocks provision for the Body of Christ.

Any reference about money unlocks fury, criticism, and unparallel scrutiny of your own life and faults. Yet, the Body of Christ remains impoverished, intimidated and...blind to the Scriptural promise of Financial Rewards.

6 Keys Every Minister Should Remember About Offerings

1.   **Recognize The Importance Of An Offering To God.** Think of many Scriptures where God carefully explains the value and future of the sowing of His people. He even listed various kinds of offerings such as the trespass offering, the peace offering, the sin offering and even the tithe! (Read Malachi 3:8-12.)

2.   **Recognize That The Offerings Of Your People Are Deciding Their Future.** Their Seeds determine their Harvest. Your ministry and celebration of their Seed will affect their opinion of their giving. "Honour the Lord with thy substance, and with the firstfruits of all thine increase: So shall thy barns be filled with plenty, and thy presses shall burst out with new wine," (Proverbs 3:9-10).

3.   **Teach Your People To Treasure The Moment Of Sowing.** Jesus stood and watched the widow give all she had. (See Mark 12:41-44.) God assigned a prophet to one widow just to help her

unlock the Seed for her Harvest. (Read 1 Kings 17.)

4. **Remember That Any Attention You Give To The Seeds Of The People Affects Their View Of Its Importance.** When you make statements like, "I wish we never had to receive offerings," you have just belittled and possibly destroyed the *impact* of their Seed.

5. **Make The Moment Of Bringing An Offering To God An Unforgettable Portrait Of Blessing In The Hearts Of Your Families.** One of my dear friends in Pennsylvania has an event at every service during the offering. He places several offering containers on the steps of the platform. Each family comes as a unit, standing at the offering container and praying together over their Seed. When they have finished praying over their Seed, they place it in the offering container and return to their seats. Then, the next family moves up behind them. There are several rows of people giving. It is a most holy, sacred and *unforgettable* moment of receiving offerings.

6. **Never Rush The Offering Of The People To Their God.** You do not rush the choir. You do not rush the announcement about the baseball games. Why would you rush the *Thanksgiving Moment* that occurs only three times in a seven day period?

Give Attention To The Offerings Of Your People.

It is One of the Secrets of the Uncommon Minister.

What Are Your Personal Persuasions About Financial Blessings?

You Can Only Reproduce What You Are. This Sunday morning you will address your congregation, or if you are an evangelist, you will be in a crusade. You will pour out your heart, preach, pray and exhaust your body and life in helping others get a Harvest they are pursuing. You will probably talk to them about receiving forgiveness for their sins, healing for their body, restoration for their marriage, a new job that they need.

If you preach miracles, blessings, and answers to prayer without ever telling them the formula, you have wasted your time and theirs! I see it happen every week. I see ministers straining, sweating, toiling, laboring, crying, weeping...trying to help their people get a Harvest. At the same time, they neglect to instruct them and teach them *how* to sow their Seeds *toward a desired Harvest.* That is the importance of understanding the Seed-Faith Principle.

7 Thoughts About The Power Of Being Persuaded

1.   **Everyone Knows That You Will Eventually Reap What You Sow.** What too few know is that you can order your Harvest in advance, if you will dare use the Seed-Faith that God has given you. (See 1 Kings 17:8-16.)

2.   **You Cannot Reproduce What You Yourself Are Not.** I doubt that you will ever hear of a horse giving birth to a pig, or an apple tree producing peaches. It is a Scriptural principle that everything will reproduce after its own kind. (See Genesis 1:11-12.)

3.   **What You Are, You Will Eventually Create Around You.** Since I am an Irishman, I will create and reproduce Irishmen. If I were a German, I would reproduce Germans. If I am a watermelon, I will create watermelons. If I am a giver, I will *reproduce* givers around me.

4.   **You Are The Seed That Controls Your Climate...Your Atmosphere.** That is exactly what Jesus taught in Luke 6:38, "Give, and it shall be given unto you; good measure, pressed down and shaken together, and running over, shall men give into your bosom."

God has always been a *giver.* I do not control the nature of God. He is a *giving God.* He is a *healing God.* He is a *loving God.* I do not change Him. What I do control are the *Entry Points of His miracles* and *blessings* and *provisions* into my life.

Just as God multiplied the meal, the food of the widow in 1 Kings 17, He could not give until she *released her Seed and became a giver!*

5.   **God Will Not Multiply What He Does Not Possess.** The little boy with five loaves and two fishes held the lunch. The multitudes were hungry. Yet, nobody was fed. Not until he gave his lunch to Jesus. (See John 6:5-13.)

6.   **What You Talk About The Most Reveals What You Love The Most...**Your children, football, the Bible, giving.

7.   **When You Talk To Your People With Enthusiasm And Excitement About Sowing And Giving To God, It Will Become Contagious In Their Hearts As Well.**

Are You A Giver? Does your family think of you as a giver? Does your church consider you generous?

If so, you will inevitably *reproduce a congregation of Seed-sowing...generous people.*

Be Persuaded.

It is One of the Secrets of the Uncommon Minister.

⚮ 8 ⚮

CREATE THE HABIT OF LISTENING TO SCRIPTURE DAILY

Listening Is Different Than Reading.

You cannot read and do other things at the same time. Reading requires total *focus*. You have to move away from everything else that you are doing.

However, listening can begin the moment you awaken. This is powerful. While you are washing your face, *you can receive the words of Jesus* into your spirit. While you are shaving, taking a bath or making up your bed, you can receive His words into the soil of your mind. Most of us take an hour or so to birth our day. That is 60 minutes that the holy words of God could be *washing your mind*.

His Word *cleanses*. (See John 15:3.)

His Word *energizes*. (See Psalm 119:149, 156.)

His Word is *life*. (See John 6:63.)

His Word *purges and purifies*. (See Psalm 119:9.)

His Word *corrects you*. (See 2 Timothy 3:16.)

His Word *warns*. (See Psalm 19:11.)

His Word *brings peace*. (See Psalm 119:165.)

His Word births *an invisible joy* that cannot be explained by anyone. (See John 15:11.)

Here is what has happened in my own life. Sometimes, I become so busy I delay taking my Bible and reading quietly in my Secret Place. I "explain" to the Lord that I will meet with Him later "when I can really concentrate and not be distracted by anything else." (This procrastination has cost me dearly.)

Listening to Scriptures on cassette tapes or your ipod solves that problem *immediately*. Satan can throw many things at you, but The Word of God is *still washing* your mind, because of your *daily* habit of listening.

4 Things To Remember About Listening To Scripture

1.   **Listening Is Not A Substitution For Reading.** You need *both*. *His Word always creates marvelous results,* regardless of how you receive it into your spirit. I have found that keeping my ipod with me in hotel rooms, next to my bed and in my automobile really influences me.

2.   **Keep CDs Or Your Ipod In Your Car.** They will discourage boring conversationalists who talk about trivia and other unimportant things. Also, it makes it possible to hear His Word separate from the clutter of business and home chores.

3.   **Keep Your Ipod Or Tapes Next To Your Bed.** Sometimes, when I am having difficulty sleeping, I will punch "play" on my ipod and listen to the Scriptures. Words cannot describe how instantly an atmosphere and climate can change in your bedroom when The Word of God fills up every corner!

4.   **Keep CDs On Your Desk At Your Church.** Using your headphones, you will always find an opportunity to receive His Word into your spirit.

▶   *Your ministry will change* in direct proportion to the Words you are hearing from Him.

▶   *Your personal joy* will be proportionate to the Words you are hearing from Him.

▶   *Your people will change* proportionate to the passion you birth in them for The Word of God.

Nobody else can do this for you. You must pursue The Word of God for yourself. Today.

Somebody has said that it takes 56 hours to read the entire Bible through. Whatever it takes, do it. Do it today. Concentrate on developing this habit. His Word is the most important thing you will hear today.

It will change you and your ministry forever.

Create The Habit Of Listening To Scripture Daily.

It is One of the Secrets of the Uncommon Minister.

≈ 9 ≈

INSIST ON ACCURACY IN YOUR PREACHING

Accuracy Really Does Matter.

Moses built the tabernacle. However, the Golden Key was his accuracy in obedience to the pattern God gave him.

Noah built the ark. Yet the Golden Key was building it *accurately,* according to the command.

Solomon built the temple. The important ingredient was building it *according to the pattern* that The Holy Spirit gave to David and him.

The Pharisees prayed. Even so, their prayers were worthless. You see, it is not enough to simply pray. You must pray according to the will of God. The Pharisees fasted. However, Jesus revealed a different set of instructions regarding the power of fasting. Attitude was everything.

7 Keys To Inspire Pursuit Of Accuracy

1.   The Uncommon Minister Must Invest The Time And Effort To Be Accurate Every Time He Ministers.

Several years ago, a real tragedy occurred for a well-known ministry. The young man carried a real anointing on his ministry. He was expressive. Fiery. Opinionated. Purposeful. One day, he threw out some so-called facts and illustrations that were later proven libelous. He was sued for a huge amount of money. Though a settlement out of court might have occurred, it created terrible distractions for himself, his staff and his ministry. He lost many partners who did not really understand the warfare against him. His attention to *accuracy* would have prevented this tragic interruption and distraction in his ministry.

I was once told that a well-known comedian had died. I used it for an illustration that night in the message only to find out later my source was completely wrong. He was still alive! It made me look like a fool and even sowed Seeds of doubt about the rest of my information to that congregation!

2.   **Verify Your Facts, Illustrations And Statistics.** Yes, it will require additional time, effort and possibly even research assistance. However, it will keep a purity and believability to your message in the long-term.

3.   **Confirm That Any Scripture You Use To Prove Your Point Really Does Prove What You Are Saying.** I remember an outstanding minister pointing this out years ago in a camp meeting. It really registered with me, though I was just a teenage boy of fifteen. Someone had said that Jesus left 99 sheep "in the fold." The minister pointed out that the Bible did not say that at all. Jesus asked, "What man of you, having an hundred sheep, if he lose one of them, doth not leave the ninety and nine *in the wilderness*, and go after that which is lost, until he find it?" (Luke 15:4).

I have heard ministers use quotations from Shakespeare and say that they were in the "Scriptures." They were not.

It is very easy to confuse well-known sayings as Scriptures. *Confirm* them before using them.

4.   **When You Are Uncertain About The Material, Avoid Using It, Or Announce Your Uncertainty About The Information.** Obviously, when you are doing private Bible studies or midweek services, your spontaneity would be too stifled to avoid referencing completely. However, always provide yourself a *verbal disclaimer* by mentioning that "someone told me, though I have not confirmed it."

Your feelings are not facts.

5.   **Your Credibility Is Inseparable From Your Believability.** It is so important that your people feel comfortable in believing what you are speaking. *Trust Is Your Greatest Gift To Others.*

6.   **Always Distinguish To People Between Something You Are Feeling As A Man Of God, And Something God Actually Spoke To You.** Ministers have been known to look at someone and say, "Your husband is coming back home to you. Relax and believe God." Yet, that husband married someone else and never did return to the marriage. It devastated the lady who was hoping

the "so-called" prophecy of the minister was correct.

The path of Christianity is filled with wounded bodies of hopeful believers who trusted the word of a man of God who simply had a *feeling* about a situation, not a true *word* from God.

Intuition is not always the Voice of The Spirit.

7.   The Uncommon Minister Must Protect The Hope Of Others. Their hope must be in The Word *of God,* not merely the fleeting feelings of the man of God. Pastors are faced with this much more often than traveling ministries. Many pastors have spent hours rebuilding the broken hopes of their people months after a traveling evangelist left who had "a special word from God."

It is obvious you want to be an Uncommon Minister. That is why you are reading this book. I urge you to learn the huge difference between your feelings and a true word from God *for* you or *through* you.

Insist On Accuracy In Your Preaching.

It is One of the Secrets of the Uncommon Minister.

Go Where You
   Are Celebrated Instead
Of Where You
   Are Tolerated.

-MIKE MURDOCK

⇚ **10** ⇚

LEARN FROM THE UNHAPPY VOICES AROUND YOU

━━━━━━►►-O-◄◄━━━━━━

Never Trivialize The Disappointments Of Others.

Unhappy People Often Birth Uncommon Ideas. When you read the biography of great businesses, they always include the *complaints* of customers. Those complaints created changes, correction and ultimately, uncommon profits. Every extraordinary business champion states clearly, *"Listen to your customers.* They will tell you the problems that require solving."

One of the most respected ministers in my life is my dear friend, Sherman Owens, from Sarasota, Florida. I will never forget his teaching: "Listen to happy voices for encouragement. Listen to unhappy voices for *ideas."*

7 Things To Remember About Learning From The Unhappy

1.   Joseph Understood The Secret Of Studying The Unhappy. It was the secret of his promotion to the palace. *Compassion* was his *dominant* gift. When he noticed the downcast faces of two prisoners, he inquired and pursued an explanation. The butler and baker for Pharaoh explained their dreams. Joseph interpreted those dreams accurately. Two years later, Joseph was remembered by the butler for responding to his sorrowful countenance and dream. Joseph became Prime Minister within 24 hours. (Read Genesis 40-41.)

Your Reactions Determine Who Pursues You.
▶ You need *Encouraging* Voices to strengthen you.
▶ You need *Mentoring* Voices to avoid mistakes.

► You need *Unhappy* Voices for *creativity* and *ideas.*

2.   Listen To The Unhappy In Your Church. People are rarely angry for the reason they tell you. The *unspoken* must be pursued. The *unexpressed* must be given time and a season for expression. Take the time to inquire. Listen *without judgment.* Permit others to express their views, fears and feelings. Was there a *broken* promise? Unfilled *expectations?* I still have a deep problem with those who make promises and continuously change them.

Children find it almost impossible to deal with the burden of an unkept promise by their parents.

► *Unexpressed* disappointment often becomes silent *rage.*
► Silent rage often births *retaliation* and a strategy to *destroy.*
► You cannot afford to permit The Unhappy to linger in that condition. Depression, suicide and even murder have been the result.

3.   Listen To The Unhappy On Your Staff. What is the real reason for their lack of joy? *You cannot solve a problem that you do not see.* The doctor cannot heal a wound he has not discovered. The lawyer cannot win a case that he does not understand.

Each moment of *listening* moves you closer to the Miracle of Solution.

4.   Never Assume You Understand The Real Cause Of Sorrows, Despondency Or Anger Within Others. Let me explain. I dearly loved a young couple that worked for me. Continuously, I looked for ways to bless them and encourage them. Occasionally, I would press a large bill in his hand at the airport and say, "Take your wife out to supper tonight." Yet, their agitation persisted. Nothing was ever enough for them. After much thought, listening and study of their life, I discovered the following elements:

► They refused pastoral mentorship and faithful attendance to a local church.
► They refused to follow the principles of success that I taught them privately.
► They refused to attend sessions on financial prosperity held within minutes of their home.

Nothing you can say will satisfy the heart of the disobedient.

5.   Many Pastors Could Have Retained And Kept Disgruntled Sheep Had They Invested The Appropriate Time To Listen Long Enough To Understand Them And Their Pain. On the other hand, many pastors would stop blaming themselves had they understood the deep-rooted problem in unhappy church members.

6.   The Best Preacher On Earth Cannot Solve The Problem Of The Unteachable. *The Unteachable Always Remain Unhappy.* That is why Jesus never pursued Pharisees. He never visited them when they were sick. Jesus went where He was desired, not where He was needed. Wisdom Key #38: *Go Where You Are Celebrated Instead Of Where You Are Tolerated.*

7.   Do Not Invest More Time In The Unhappy Than You Do Those Who Are Supportive And Encouraging To You. Too often, those who bless us are ignored. The satisfied are overlooked. The obnoxious often receive far too much time, energy and attention. Be sensitive. That is why Jesus never gave long answers to Pharisees. He saved His time for Zacchaeus and the woman at the well—those who qualified for the Seed of His Attention.

It is not the responsibility of the Uncommon Minister to solve every problem for everyone around him. Jesus did not try. You cannot do it. You are human. Accept that. Do only what you are instructed by The Holy Spirit to do.

But, you can *Learn* From *ANY* Environment.

Learn From The Unhappy Voices Around You. It is One of the Secrets of the Uncommon Minister.

What You Say Is Not As Important As What Others Remember.

-MIKE MURDOCK

⮾ 11 ⮾

NEVER DISCUSS IN THE PULPIT ANYTHING YOU WANT OTHERS TO FORGET

━━━━━➤ﱢ◉ﱬ◀━━━━━

Your Words Are Pictures.
Unforgettable pictures.

Your words enable thoughts to become permanent. It is dangerous to speak about things that do not really matter. Your words give life and longevity to *anything* discussed.

Words keep many things alive. Many arguments would die; many conflicts would die. However, your *words* keep sustaining them.

8 Facts Ministers Should Remember About Their Words

1. **Your Words Breathe Life Into Everything.** "Death and life are in the power of the tongue: and they that love it shall eat the fruit thereof," (Proverbs 18:21).

2. **Your Words Can Wound.** "The words of a talebearer are as wounds, and they go down into the innermost parts of the belly," (Proverbs 18:8).

3. **Your Words Can Create Conflict.** "A fool's lips enter into contention, and his mouth calleth for strokes," (Proverbs 18:6).

4. **Your Words Can Destroy A Lifetime Friendship In A Moment.** "A froward man soweth strife: and a whisperer separateth chief friends," (Proverbs 16:28).

5. **Your Right Words Can Breathe Health Into A Frail Body.** "Pleasant words are as an honeycomb, sweet to the soul, and health to the bones," (Proverbs 16:24). "A wholesome tongue is a tree of life," (Proverbs 15:4).

6.   The Results Of Your Entire Ministry Will Be Impacted By The Words You Select. "A man hath joy by the answer of his mouth: and a word spoken in due season, how good is it!" (Proverbs 15:23).

7.   You Should Never Stay In The Presence Of People Speaking Wrong Words. "Go from the presence of a foolish man, when thou perceivest not in him the lips of knowledge," (Proverbs 14:7).

8.   Any Inappropriate Words You Speak Will Often Be Remembered Longer Than Appropriate Words. Several years ago, a minister had a devastating experience. False accusations were hurled at him. Emotionally shattered, he shared the experience publicly with some of his congregation. Most of them knew nothing about the false accusations, *until he had brought them out publicly.* It simply created more questions in their mind. Tiny doubts grew like small plants.

"Were they really true after all? Maybe there is another side to the story? Is he telling us *everything?*"

One by one, his supporters dissolved. Yes, the accusations were proven later to be false. However, the damage was done.

He had painted scenarios in their mind that time could not erase. His words were photographs that satan could nurture, feed and grow *in the privacy of their imagination.*

A pastor in South Louisiana brought me to a beautiful home of a well-known evangelist many years ago. His wife came out and welcomed us warmly. When she disappeared in the back of the house to call for her husband, the pastor turned to me and said, "She was married to a famous baseball manager several years ago. Now, she is married to this evangelist."

I was stunned. When she came back, that thought dominated my mind. She was warm and kind. The conversation was pleasant. Yet, in the coming days, every time I thought of this evangelist and his wife, I pictured her as married to this famous baseball manager.

A few days later, the pastor and I were driving together again. Suddenly, he said, "Oh, I made a mistake about that wife of the preacher a few days ago. I got her mixed up with someone else. She was not married to anyone else before this evangelist."

The picture was already in concrete. That happened 25 years ago, and I am sitting here tonight in my Wisdom Room thinking about this couple. In my mind, she is still married to that baseball manager. The Seed has never quit growing.

You cannot stop everyone from discussing you. Even so, *never provide them information you want them to forget...Nothing.*

Never give *unnecessary* information that requires, demands or inspires pursuit of undesirable questions.

Be cautious in confessing your mistakes publicly. Your attempts to "be open" may be very sincere. Yet, your mistake may loom bigger *in their memory* than the lesson you are trying to teach from it. Wisdom Key #80: *What You Say Is Not As Important As What Others Remember.*

People often remember illustrations for the wrong reasons.

Never Discuss In The Pulpit Something You Want Others To Forget.

It is One of the Secrets of the Uncommon Minister.

RECOMMENDED INVESTMENTS:
Seeds of Wisdom on The Power of Words, Volume 26 (Book/B-128/
  32 Pages/$5)
Seeds of Wisdom on Bitterness, Volume 36 (Book/B-203/32 Pages/$5)

Anything
Permitted
Increases.

-MIKE MURDOCK

❧ 12 ❧

IDENTIFY AND REMOVE CONTENTIOUS PEOPLE INVOLVED IN YOUR MINISTRY

Conflict Distracts.

Every minister knows this. When a staff member cannot get along with others, unity and productivity are diminished. Focus is broken. Projects are delayed. The spiritual progress of an entire church can be paralyzed.

Nothing is more harmful to your ministry than a contentious person. A contentious person often considers himself very honest and up front. In fact, they take pride in telling you "the way things really are." Subconsciously, they are often modeling someone in their life (a father or mother) who accomplished their goals through *intimidation.* They admire this person and have decided to follow that pattern.

Unfortunately, they fail to see the *losses* created.

13 Facts Every Minister Should Recognize About Contentious People

1.   **Contentious People Often Destroy The Momentum, Bonding And Synergy That Unity Creates.** "Mark them which cause divisions and offences...avoid them." (Read Romans 16:17; 2 Timothy 2:24.)

2.   **Contentious People Destroy The Rewards Of Agreement, The Greatest Law Of Success On Earth.** "Two are better than one; because they have a good reward for their labour. For if they fall, the one will lift up his fellow: but woe to him that is alone when he falleth; for he hath not another to help him up," (Ecclesiastes 4:9-10).

3. **The True Character Of A Contentious Person Is Rarely Revealed Until You Rebuke Them.** If he is a scorner and fool, he will hate you. If he is a wise person simply needing correction, he will love you. "Reprove not a scorner, lest he hate thee: rebuke a wise man, and he will love thee," (Proverbs 9:8).

4. **You Can Succeed Almost Anywhere Else, Except With A Contentious Person.** Solomon experienced this. "It is better to dwell in the corner of the housetop, than with a brawling woman and in a wide house," (Proverbs 25:24).

5. **Contentious People Openly Break Confidences Of Others.** "He that passeth by, and meddleth with strife belonging not to him, is like one that taketh a dog by the ears," (Proverbs 26:17).

6. **A Contentious Person Enjoys Debate, Disputing And Opposing.** A contentious person always looks for a reason to disagree. They *ignore* every point of *agreement*.

7. **A Contentious Person Is Always The Entrance For Satan To Launch Every Evil Work In Your Ministry.** "For where envying and strife is, there is confusion and every evil work," (James 3:16).

8. **A Contentious Person Is The Opposite Of A Wise Person.** "But the Wisdom that is from above is first pure, *then peaceable*, gentle, and *easy to be intreated*, full of mercy and good fruits, without partiality, and without hypocrisy," (James 3:17).

9. **A Contentious Attitude Is Contagious And Wounds Many.** When someone permits the spirit of conflict to enter their life, they will affect *everyone around them*. I have seen a peaceful household turn to argument thirty minutes after someone entered the room. Happy congregations become chaotic and embittered when one "talebearer" joins the church.

10. **Unthankfulness Is The Seed That Births A Contentious Attitude.** It is the sin that God abhors. It was the *first* sin. Satan was unthankful for his position and chose to fight for dominion.

11. **Ingratitude Is The Season Before Conflict.** It can destroy a family within weeks. It can ruin a successful ministry within months. Churches exploding with growth have been fragmented within weeks when a spirit of ingratitude invaded the congregation.

12. Contentious People Often Sabotage The Work Of God. Many years ago I heard one of the most startling statements from a famous missionary. I was sitting under some huge trees in East Africa. Monkeys were jumping from limb to limb.

"Mike, the number one reason missionaries do not stay on the mission field is their *inability to get along with the other missionaries working in their same territory.*"

Think about it. Missionaries who should stay in love with Jesus, obsessed with bringing the Gospel to the lost, return home *because of arguments* and the failure to create harmony and an environment of agreement.

13. Any Contentious Person Who Refuses To Change Must Be Removed. "Where no wood is, there the fire goeth out: so where there is no talebearer, the strife ceaseth. As coals are to burning coals, and wood to fire; so is a contentious man to kindle strife. The words of a talebearer are as wounds, and they go down into the innermost parts of the belly," (Proverbs 26:20-22).

Stop *any* conversation birthing contention. Immediately speak up and interrupt the conversation with statements like, "Oh, it is wonderful how God will *turn this* for our good! I am so thankful for what God is about to do in this situation! We have a wonderful God!" It will be like throwing cold water on a destructive fire. Wisdom Key #25: *Anything Permitted Increases.*

Boldly confront the contentious about their attitude. Others are bold enough to *poison* your atmosphere and climate with arrows of unthankfulness piercing the air. Dominate your turf. Take charge. Use your words to turn the tide.

Agreement is one of the greatest enemies satan fears.

Identify And Remove Contentious People Involved In Your Ministry.

It is One of the Secrets of the Uncommon Minister.

RECOMMENDED INVESTMENTS:
The Wisdom Commentary, Volume 1 (Book/B-136PB/256 Pages/$25)
The Wisdom Commentary, Volume 2 (Book/B-220PB/312 Pages/$25)

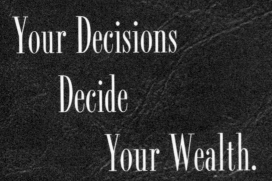

Your Decisions
Decide
Your Wealth.

-MIKE MURDOCK

❧ 13 ❧

SECURE THE BEST OFFICE EQUIPMENT POSSIBLE FOR YOUR MINISTRY

―――――⬦――――

Proper Equipment Increases Your Productivity.
I am holding in my hand a digital recorder. You see, I can speak six times faster than I can write. If one of my staff was sitting here receiving my dictation, I would be tying up their time for hours. My associate would have to wait for me, time would be wasted and I would feel the pressure of producing and making their moments count. Instead, this digital recorder frees them to finish other tasks. Proper machines really help.

Never have someone do a job that a machine can do instead. There are numerous and wonderful reasons for this. Machines cannot think and make judgments in flexible situations. Humans can. So, I try to free the time of my staff as much as possible to do those things, and use the machines to do other tasks.

Enjoy these Ten Humorous Reasons for using proper machines.

10 Reasons To Invest In Quality Equipment

1.   **Machines Do Not Require Coaxing, Merely Repair.**
2.   **Machines Do Not Get Discouraged And Disheartened When Their Mother-In-Law Comes To Town.**
3.   **Machines Are Never Disloyal, Discussing Your Secrets With Everyone Else.**
4.   **Your Machines Will Not File Grievance Reports Against You With Employment Commissions When You Fail To Meet Their Expectations.**
5.   **Machines Do Not Require Medical Insurance, Sick Leave And Time Off.**

6. **Machines Can Be Replaced Quickly And Easily.**

7. **Machines Do Not Request A Retirement Fund And Want To Be Paid For The Years Ahead When They Cannot Perform.**

8. **Machines Never Come To Work Late And Then Ask To Leave Early.**

9. **Machines Will Work Through Lunch, Requiring No "Break Time."**

10. **Machines Never Interrupt The Productivity Of Other Machines When They Are Not Being Used.**

This was not my philosophy in my early ministry. In fact, I often refused to purchase expensive equipment. Consequently, it increased the load on my staff. Looking back, this was ludicrous. Yet, at the time, I felt like it provided work for more staff people. Now, I recognize that people are needed to *supervise* the machines and equipment. This increases their own productivity and worth.

That is why I continuously instruct my staff:

▶ *Find the most effective equipment possible to do your present job.* Telephone other businesses or ministries. Attend seminars and workshops. Whatever it takes to do your job more efficiently, more accurately and quickly—tell me. I will do anything possible to make the hours of my employees more effective and productive.

▶ *Continuously evaluate your productivity.* What machine could make a big difference in the completion of your daily tasks and responsibilities. What is slowing you down?

▶ *Present me with options to your present equipment.* When you become computer-minded, equipment oriented and aware of the remarkable inventions of our day, you will increase the productivity of your ministry dramatically. Your staff will treasure it and learn to appreciate their own work load reduction because of it. It decreases their opportunities for mistakes. It increases the standardization of their work.

Secure The Best Office Equipment Possible For Your Ministry.
It is One of the Secrets of the Uncommon Minister.

≈ 14 ≈

VALUE THE VOWS OF YOUR PEOPLE

Vows Matter Greatly To God.

Vows are not playful moments.

Vows are the catalyst for miracles. "When thou vowest a vow unto God, defer not to pay it; for He hath no pleasure in fools: pay that which thou hast vowed. Better is it that thou shouldest not vow, than that thou shouldest vow and not pay," (Ecclesiastes 5:4-5).

Promise Breakers Are *Fools.*

Promise Makers Are *Wise.*

Promise Keepers Are *Rewarded.* Always.

4 Facts Every Minister Should Know About Vows And Covenants

1. **God Is A Covenant God.** He makes agreements and contracts with those who honor His integrity.

2. **Uncommon Champions Often Make Uncommon Vows To God.** One of the most effective mentors I know made a vow to God. He believed that he would die unless he kept that vow. He told God that if He would heal him, he would preach this Gospel the rest of his life. He kept that vow and blessed millions. God always guarantees blessings to those who observe and "do all His commandments," (see Deuteronomy 28:1).

3. **Vows Will Often Emerge During The Season Of A Special Anointing Or Challenge Of Faith By A Man Of God.** I was sitting at the table with one of my dear mentors. Suddenly, The Holy Spirit rose up strong for me to sow an unforgettable and uncommon Seed into his life. Why? The anointing upon him was the *magnet* that unleashed my own faith.

While sitting in a conference, a man of God challenged the ministers present to plant an unusual Seed. My heart leaped. I sowed the Seed and experienced an incredible encounter with The Holy Spirit less than thirty days later.

4. Encourage Your People To Keep Their Vows To The Work Of God. Do not be discouraged when many vows are not kept. Everyone requires teaching. Everyone becomes discouraged.

Recently, a pastor friend lamented the lack of follow through on the Faith-Promises of people. He was agitated and almost critical.

"Many of my people are not completing their faith-promises. Thousands of dollars are promised to the work of God, and they are not completing these vows."

I inquired, "Think for a moment. What did you do following the service when they came forward to the altar and made those Faith-Promises?"

Total silence. He had done *nothing*. I explained patiently to him that when anyone comes into the presence of God, their faith will ignite. Hope leaps. Doubt evaporates. When your people come into the presence of God, they receive *glimpses* of their next season. They are ecstatic, stirred and excited. Remember, when the Israelites received an inward photograph of Canaan, their energy exploded. Life becomes exciting because of the *dominant* picture in your heart.

"When your people left the church service, that experience of Anointing was attacked," I explained. "They entered the world of their business, television reports and relatives who voiced doubt, sarcasm and even unbelief. Their faith always takes a beating following their step toward God."

He was puzzled, but I continued. "When your people make Faith-Promises, they are reacting to the supernatural presence of God. The Holy Spirit has spoken to their heart. They respond to His voice with acts of faith. When they return to their homes, the climate changes. The atmosphere becomes adversarial. Their families bicker, quarrel and even become angry over their step of faith. Many of your people endure sarcastic words from relatives about the church, prosperity preachers and televangelists."

I encouraged him to remember this and *Value The Vows Of His People.*

≈ 15 ≈

MAKE SURE THE VOICE OF GOD IS THE FIRST VOICE YOU HEAR EVERY MORNING

His Voice Is The Only Voice That Truly Matters.

Your people are trusting. They lean on you. They depend on you. However, your words will not bless and strengthen them *unless you have heard from God yourself.*

You will not have the patience and endurance to handle *their* crisis unless you hear the voice of God yourself. Wisdom Key #251: *What You Hear Determines What You Pursue.*

Your people cannot *talk* to God for you.

Your people cannot *know* the voice of God for you.

The psalmist discovered this, "O God, Thou art my God; early will I seek Thee: my soul thirsteth for Thee, my flesh longeth for Thee in a dry and thirsty land, where no water is; To see Thy power and Thy glory, so as I have seen Thee in the sanctuary," (Psalm 63:1-2).

What You Hear First Determines What You Speak Next. One of the ingredients of the perfect day includes hearing the voice of God each morning.

You Must Hear His Voice *Before You Hear The Bad News About The Economy.* He has promised supernatural provision. "Thou wilt keep him in perfect peace, whose mind is stayed on Thee: because he trusteth in Thee," (Isaiah 26:3).

You Must Hear His Voice *Before The Report Of The Doctor Comes.* God is your great physician. "Great peace have they which love Thy law: and nothing shall offend them," (Psalm 119:165).

You Must Hear His Voice *Before Others Have Had An Opportunity To Influence You.* He alone knows the truth.

After You Hear The Voice Of God, *The Critical Words Of Others Have Little Effect Upon You.* His presence reassures you.

His words correct your course. His peace settles the storms within you.

After You Hear His Words, The *Flattering Words Of Others Cannot Puff You Up*. Both feet are on the ground. Your instructions are clear.

After You Hear The Voice Of God, *You Will Not Require The Praise Of Others*. His confidence in you satisfies completely.

After You Hear The Voice Of God, *Your Attitude Will Change Instantly*. You will not face the future with anger, torment or fear. He has spoken. His Words have settled every issue. Time will prove Him correct.

That is why listening to cassettes of the Scriptures is so important. *Every morning.* Without fail. Keep them in your car. Keep them beside your bed. Keep them in your office. Encourage your entire family to absorb The Word of God *daily* by cassette. Nothing you could give another could surpass the Bible on cassette tape. His Words are forever settled in Heaven.

When you awaken, everything else often seems so urgent. Each phone call appears desperate. Every letter on your desk screams for attention. Everybody has a deserving request.

You will never create order until you make His presence your priority. Wisdom Key #148: *The Holy Spirit Is The Only Person You Are Required To Obey.*

10 Reasons You Should Hear The Voice Of God First

1. **Hear His Voice Before You Return Any Phone Calls To Those In Trouble.** Why? You will not know how to respond properly until you have The Mentor's Manna. Each day will require a fresh anointing for the different needs of your ministry.

2. **Hear His Voice Before You Answer Any Letters.** Why? You may make wrong commitments and promises you cannot fulfill. Respond to His *commands* instead of the needs of people.

3. **Hear His Voice Before You Listen To The Voices Of Others.** Why? Their *problems* are driving them, while the *plan of God* should be wooing you. Others are driven by their needs. You must be *led* by the commands of God.

4. **Hear His Voice Before You Listen To The Complaints**

Of Others. Why? His peace will keep you. He can calm your spirit and rest your mind. You are not responsible for the happiness of others. That is a work of The Spirit.

5.   **Hear His Voice Before You Embrace The Ideas Of Others.** Why? The *ideas* of men are *not* the *commands* of God. The doubts and fears of people are like magnets. They attach themselves to your spirit dragging you down like the barnacles on a ship. You become emotionally paralyzed by carrying around their "baggage."

6.   **Hear His Voice Before Responding To Any Requests Of Others.** Why? You must *qualify the soil* before you give to someone. Your Seed is precious. The Seed of your Time, Love or Money deserves a *screening process.* Do not sow everything into everyone. *Qualify the soil.* Stony ground? Thorny ground? It is so easy to be persuaded by people. Wrong people. Oh, how I wish I could go back and change some of the Seed-sowing that I have done! I allowed the faces of people to affect my Seed-sowing. Some have cried "crocodile tears." I was affected. On more than one occasion, I have emptied my pockets to someone who was actually *unqualified* to receive. Why? I had not been in His presence to hear His voice. *Good Seed Deserves Good Soil.*

7.   **Hear His Voice Before Revealing Your Dreams Or Discoveries To Others.** Why? When the wrong people hear your dreams, they can sabotage your faith for them. *When Satan Wants To Destroy You, He Puts A Person Close To You.* A wrong person. Wrong people sow Seeds of doubt and unbelief.

8.   **Hear His Voice Before You Pursue The Approval Of Others.** Why? Pride can destroy you. Praise feeds pride. "These six things doth the Lord hate: yea, seven are an abomination unto Him: A proud look, a lying tongue. An heart that deviseth wicked imaginations, feet that be swift in running to mischief, A false witness that speaketh lies, and he that soweth discord among brethren," (Proverbs 6:16-19).

Praise is often excessive, cunning and deceptive. It is often used to manipulate ministers into an intimate relationship or an unwise decision. Flattery is satanic. Hearing His voice *protects you* from these arrows that fly relentlessly toward your life.

9.   **Hear His Voice Before Absorbing Disturbing News Reports.** "I rejoice at Thy Word, as one that findeth great spoil," (Psalm 119:162).

"Great peace have they which love Thy law: and nothing shall offend them," (Psalm 119:165).

"Thou wilt keep him in perfect peace, whose mind is stayed on Thee: because he trusteth in Thee," (Isaiah 26:3).

10. Hear His Voice Before Making Significant Changes In Your Ministry.

You were never given the responsibility of planning your ministry.

You were given the responsibility of *discovering His plan* for your ministry.

Make Sure The Voice Of God Is The First Voice You Hear Every Morning.

It is One of the Secrets of the Uncommon Minister.

RECOMMENDED INVESTMENTS:
The Holy Spirit Handbook (Book/B-100/153 Pages/$15)
The Greatest Day of My Life (Book/B-116/32 Pages/$7)
The Strategy of Hourly Obedience (6 Tapes/TS-08/$30)
The School of The Holy Spirit, Series 1: The Greatest Secret of The Universe
(6 Tapes/TS-50/$30)

≈ 16 ≈

GIVE AN ALTAR CALL IN EVERY SERVICE

───▶▷·◦·◁◀───

An Altar Call Is A Door To Change.

An altar call is your personal invitation to others to respond specifically to the message you have just ministered.

In my early ministry, I remember the pastor coming up to conclude a service after I had ministered. He would simply ask, "How many people tonight need to accept Christ as your personal Savior?" As I sat there embarrassed and humiliated, I watched many come to Christ under the pastor's personal invitation, because I was too focused on my teaching rather than their decision about the message.

14 Important Keys Every Minister Should Know About Altar Calls

1. Preaching Requires A Decision. Imagine a lawyer spending hours presenting a case in a court and then walking out without ever asking the jury for a verdict! Imagine a salesman talking about the automobile you are viewing for possible purchasing and walking away without ever asking you, "Can I write this contract up for you today?"

2. Make Altar Calls For Decisions To Follow Christ. When you preach *salvation,* you should invite those present to make a decision to follow Christ.

3. Make Altar Calls For Those Needing Healing. When you preach *healing,* you should invite those who want to experience healing to come forward and receive that miracle from God.

4. Make Altar Calls For Those Accepting Their Assignment To Enter The Ministry. When you preach *commitment* to Christian service, you should *invite* those present to come forward and dedicate their lives to be used of the Lord in His work.

5. **Appeal To The Heart, Not The Intellect, During Your Altar Call.** Explain what you are talking about in terms others can understand. Some do not understand the phrase, "Born again." Recognize that the jargon and vocabulary of every church group varies.

6. **Never Assume Everyone Present Really Understands The Gospel.** They do not. *That Which Becomes Familiar Often Becomes Hidden From Us.* We are so familiar with the Gospel that we assume everyone understands it fully.

7. **Never Schedule Too Many Things In A Service To Overlook The Most Important Thing—Accepting Jesus As Your Personal Savior.** Remember that a short altar call can often be just as effective as a long altar call. Some of my most effective altar calls have taken less than three minutes to give. The Holy Spirit was already working. I simply needed to "pull in the net."

8. **Allow The Holy Spirit Enough Time To Speak To People.** Do not rush every altar call. Great decisions sometimes require extra time. I have watched uncommon evangelists linger long during an altar call so that "just one more can come to Christ." Some of the greatest conversions on earth have taken place in the last few seconds of a lingering altar call.

9. **Listen Continuously For The Timing Of The Holy Spirit Regarding Your Altar Call.** God uses me in the first few minutes of a service to present an altar call. In the ministries of others, He moves differently. *Find the pattern* God provides for your own ministry and in specific services, and you will see the hand of God move miraculously in every service.

10. **Expect The Holy Spirit To Do His Work In The Hearts Of Others.** You are not the human persuader. The *Holy Spirit* persuades. You are the *presenter* of the Gospel, *not the persuader* of the message. Your message, or altar call, should present the facts necessary for a decision to be made. You must trust The Holy Spirit to do His work, in His timing, in the hearts of the people.

11. **Make Your Altar Call Easy To Understand.** I remember being in a huge church in California where the pastor gave detailed instructions. "Pick up your purse and your Bible and make

certain all your belongings are in your hand. Now, come to the front and place your feet against this platform." He was almost ridiculous in the details. Yet, over the years I discovered how important it was that the people would know exactly *why* they were coming, and *what would occur.* Explain how long you will require them to stand at the front or meet with counselors in a private room.

12. Give Enough Information To Remove Any Fears, Discomfort Or Uncertainty About The Altar Call. Recently, a pastor had visitors come forward and follow a man into a room in the back of the church for private counseling. I sat there shocked. You see, he told them to follow a man they had never seen in their life to a strange room that was uncomfortable and foreign to them for advice they never really asked for. As a visitor, I would have never followed that instruction. I would have sat down and gone back home and talked to God in my private time. It is important that you remove any potential discomfort for those responding to an altar call. (That is why I present my own altar call in a very different fashion and at the *beginning* of any service instead of the end.)

13. Give An Altar Call Anywhere And Any Time The Holy Spirit Leads You. A great preacher of many years ago, had a tragic and unforgettable experience. As he sat in a restaurant with friends, The Holy Spirit impressed him to talk to the waiter about his soul. The countenance of the waiter had stirred him. However, in an effort to keep a relaxed atmosphere, he ignored the prompting of The Holy Spirit. Approximately one-and-a-half hours later he noticed that the waiter had never returned to his table. He inquired about the waiter. The manager replied that they had just found the young man in the back of the restaurant, *hanging.* He had committed suicide during the meal. The preacher used this to encourage young ministers to always follow the leadership of The Holy Spirit in leading someone to Christ.

14. Keep Your Altar Calls Simple, Avoiding Doctrinal Controversy. There is a time for doctrinal teaching. The altar call is a time for a simple decision about experiencing God or the supernatural miracle He has promised.

Your altar call can be varied, presented creatively and at different times in a service. However, it is important that you recognize the necessity of it. *Give An Altar Call In Every Service.*

It is One of the Secrets of the Uncommon Minister.

Your Significance Is
   Not In Your Similarity
To Another, But In Your
   Point Of Difference
From Another.

-MIKE MURDOCK

❧ 17 ❧

STOP EXPECTING EVERYONE TO UNDERSTAND YOUR STYLE OF MINISTRY

⟶❥-◦-⧉⟵

Your Friends Celebrate Your Difference.

Your enemies *despise* your difference.

Your congregation has responded to your *difference,* not your similarity to other ministries.

6 Keys To Discerning Your Divine Distinction

1. God Has Made You Unlike Other Ministers For A Reason. The apostle Paul reached those that Peter could not reach. Jeremiah reached those that Jonah could not reach. Jesus chose 12 disciples, not one.

2. God Holds You Accountable For Finding Your Difference From Other Ministries. "Now there are diversities of gifts, but the same Spirit. And there are differences of administrations, but the same Lord. And there are diversities of operations, but it is the same God which worketh all in all," (1 Corinthians 12:4-6).

3. Uncommon Ministers Know That Many Will Not Respond To Them And Accept Their Ministry. One of the most effective teachers in Christianity is Dr. Frederick K. C. Price. On page 39 in his book, "Practical Suggestions for Successful Ministry," he writes, *"Only certain people listen to me.* There are people who would not cross the street to hear me. And I know this! I do not operate under any illusions. Everyone does not like my *method* of teaching; everyone is not *ready* for me; and I'm not ready for everybody. I know it and I don't sweat it. I am believing God is going to send the people to me who will respond to my kind of *personality,* my kind of *ministry,* my kind of whatever it might be."

4.   Some Ministers Have A Universal Appeal To Keep The Masses Of Humanity Aware Of God And The Bible. Billy Graham has such a ministry. Nothing in his message has been extreme. His Assignment is connected to the masses.

5.   Some Ministers Are Raised Up To Solve A Specific Problem For A Group Of People. Healing ministries are raised up for the sick. Some ministries have one focus—feeding children who are hungry. Some ministries are obsessed with freeing drug addicts from cocaine. You are assigned to someone, not *everyone*.

6.   Those Who Do Not Discern Your Difference And Gift Become Unqualified For A Relationship With You.   Do everything you can to explain your ministry effectively, thoroughly and repetitiously enough to be understood. When it is refused, "keep fishing" for those who want the message God has given you.

Major ministries will write a new friend or partner for a few weeks. Then, they suddenly stop. Why? They realize that the several letters invested were not understood, appreciated or desired by the new friend. So, they keep reaching to others who *do* want what they have.

You are not assigned to everybody.

Stop Expecting Everyone To Understand Your Style Of Ministry. It is One of the Secrets of the Uncommon Minister.

≈ 18 ≈

NEGOTIATE EVERYTHING

————————

Nothing Is Ever As It First Appears.

I walked into a luggage store here in Dallas many years ago. When I had selected the luggage I desired, I asked the young lady if she could provide a *"corporate discount."*

"What is a corporate discount?"

"Forty percent off."

"All right!" was her reply.

With one simple question, I saved several hundred dollars. *Negotiate Everything.*

While standing at the airline counter, I was informed that my excess baggage was over $200.

"I was hoping you would show me a little mercy today," I joked gently.

The agent thought for a few moments and replied, "All right." With one simple statement, I saved over $200.

▶ Your words are *making* you more money or costing you.

▶ Your words are bringing *Increase* or Decrease.

▶ Your words are creating *Doors* or Walls.

▶ Your words are *Bridges* or Barricades.

The Scriptures teach it: "A man shall eat good by the fruit of his mouth," (Proverbs 13:2). "The wicked is snared by the transgression of his lips: but the just shall come out of trouble," (Proverbs 12:13).

7 Facts You Should Remember When Negotiating With Others

1. Successful Negotiation Requires The Right Attitude. Nobody wants to be taken lightly, intimidated or pushed. Everybody is involved. The lady in the luggage store wanted to sell the luggage, create favor and a happy customer. *I gave her the information that* *would accommodate that need*—forty percent discount. I returned later to buy many other items because of the favor she showed.

The airline that gave me the excess baggage for free has since received over $100,000 of my transportation business. Negotiation should be a win-win situation for everybody involved.

2.   Successful Negotiation Requires An Understanding Of The Cost Involved For Others. Donald Trump explained why his father was so successful in negotiating prices. His father invested time in finding out *exactly what the cost was* for those he was negotiating with...so he would know exactly how far to negotiate.

3.   Successful Negotiation Requires Proper Timing. Many years ago, I was very weary when I arrived home from a meeting. The flight was tiresome. As I walked into the office, a staff member approached me.

"I have to talk to you!"

"All right. Sit down. How can I help you?"

She was very aggressive and flippant. "I need a raise!"

"Well, how much are you wanting me to increase your salary each month?" I asked.

"I need $1,000 a month raise."

I really thought she was joking. She was not. She continued, "My husband and I are moving into a new home that we have just built, and I really need the income to pay for the house."

It was so ridiculous to me, I almost laughed aloud. I advised her gently that I understood her need. Perhaps, it would be well for her to find another job where she could secure the salary she needed.

"Your present salary was created by a list of problems you chose to solve for me. Now, you want a huge increase in salary. Do you have a list of the *new* problems you will begin to solve for me?" I asked.

It never crossed her mind to solve more problems for an increase in salary.

4.   Successful Negotiation Produces Long-Term Gain, Not Short-Term Gain. The famous billionaire, Sam Walton, said he never invested in a company for where it would be in eighteen months. He invested in companies that would succeed ten years down the road. Employees can often squeeze out an extra dollar from a boss during a crisis situation. However, if it causes a wall of separation, that staff person often causes himself a deeper problem in the long-term.

5.   Successful Negotiation Should Focus On Details That Matter The Most. Several years ago, a wonderful young couple wrote me about a job. They were making $5.00 an hour. He was riding a motorcycle to a second job. He had three children and worked sixteen hours a day on two jobs at $10.00 an hour total. They were destitute. My heart went out to them. They had driven all night to meet me face-to-face for an interview. I agreed to pay him what *both* of his jobs were presently providing for working sixteen hours a day. As a gesture of caring, I provided a home, free, for some extra yard work. They were thrilled and elated. Over a period of time, I also provided furniture, dishes, clothes and even a car. They were enjoyable, so I was happy to do so.

Eventually, someone influenced them to negotiate for more, at every opportunity to "squeeze me." Every time something broke, they "squeezed me." I noticed a pattern. It became one-sided.

When you have many employees in your ministry, you cannot give everyone a raise when you desire to do so. You cannot always give a raise to them the moment they deserve it. You have to think long-term for the ministry. Something within me became agitated. So, when the oven broke down, they wanted me to replace it. I was weary of replacing everything. I requested that they pay half, and I would pay the other half. They attempted to use harsh words to negotiate with me. I am not the kind of person to respond favorably to intimidation of any sort.

I realized they were frustrated. So, I explained that they had forty-five days to go find a new house, and they could purchase it themselves. Yes, they were good people, but poor negotiators. They lost a wonderful blessing trying to squeeze me for "an extra nickel." *Do not lose dollars* trying to save pennies.

▶ *Close Doors Gently.*
   If you realize that you have to end a relationship, close doors quietly. You may have to return through them again in the coming years.

▶ *Never Burn Bridges Behind You.*
   Everybody talks. Everything you do is being discussed by those that you have not yet met. Do not schedule unnecessary conflicts in your future.

6.   Attend Negotiation Seminars, Listen To Tapes, And Secure The Counsel Of Qualified Mentors Before Doing Any

Serious Negotiation.

   7.   Successful Negotiation Requires Quality Time. Do not rush anything. Run from the salesman who insists that "this is the last day of this sale." Do not fall for it. When you return a month later, they will still deal! They need your purchase more than they need their own product. Your opinion deserves to be heard. Just make certain that it is heard at the *right time* in the *right atmosphere*...with the *right attitude.*

   Negotiate Everything.

   It is One of the Secrets of the Uncommon Minister.

RECOMMENDED INVESTMENTS:
31 Secrets for Career Success (Book/B-44/114 Pages/$10)
Secrets of the Richest Man Who Ever Lived (Book/B-99/179 Pages/$12)
26 Secrets for Effective Negotiation (6 Tapes/TS-10/$30)
The Double Diamond Principle in Millionaire Mentality (6 Tapes/TS-21/$30)

⤳ **19** ⤳

NEVER ASSUME YOUR INSTRUCTIONS ARE BEING UNDERSTOOD AND COMPLETED

━━━━━⟫▸◦◂⟪━━━━━

Confirm Everything.

I have marveled that so many have kept their jobs over the years. Few seem to *follow-through* on instructions given to them by their supervisors.

True, there are a few close to you who may have proven themselves over a long period of time. They understand you. They are diligent, aggressive and trustworthy. My own experience is that there will be *less than three people* in your life who you can consistently count on to complete your instructions without your personal supervision or follow-up.

4 Clues That Your Team Will Not Follow Your Instructions

1.   When *They* Do Not Regularly Carry Paper And Pen. Never count on any person who does not regularly carry paper and pen in their hand to follow through on something you have asked them to do. *Never.* The unlearned trust their memory for everything.

2.   When They Fail To Document The Instruction The Very Moment You Give It To Them. Some carry paper and pen, but simply nod when you give them an instruction. They do not *write* it down. They do not *document* it. They trust their memory. The instruction will be *forgotten* in their busyness and over-confidence. Bank on it.

3.   When They Ask No Additional Questions About The Assignment Or Instruction. That is another clue. Few instructions are complete at the beginning. When you ask them to telephone someone about an item, they *should* ask:

    a.   Is there a *deadline* on this?

    b.   When do you need a *report back* on the results of this telephone call?

    c.   Is there anything *additional* I should know?

When additional questions are never asked following an instruction received, *they are not giving any thought to it.*

    4.   **When They Simply Say,** *"I will try,"* They Will Not Get To *It.* The word *"try"* reveals half-heartedness...lack of passion.

5 Helpful Keys In Giving Instructions To Your Staff

    1.   **Give The Instruction To One Person Only.** When two receive it, they usually expect the other to do it.

    2.   **Document The Date You Gave The Instruction To Them.** *Deadlines convey importance.*

    3.   **Require A Specific Status Report On A Specific Date.** This shows you the progress and the expected date of completion.

    4.   **Clearly Explain The Urgency Of The Instruction And Its Importance.**

    5.   **Never Give An Instruction To Someone Unqualified To Complete It.**

Never Assume Your Instructions Are Being Understood And Completed.

It is One of the Secrets of the Uncommon Minister.

RECOMMENDED INVESTMENTS:
Seeds of Wisdom on Obedience, Volume 8 (Book/B-20/32 Pages/$3)
The Gift of Wisdom for Ministers (Book/B-90/32 Pages/$10)

⇜ 20 ⇝

KEEP A BOOK WITH YOU AT ALL TIMES

━━━━━➤❋◀━━━━━

Make Moments Count.

What you read is what you will become. Reading prevents boredom. That is why magazines and books are kept in the waiting rooms of physicians' offices and hospitals. When you bring the book of your choice with you, you can maintain a continuous flow of appropriate information into your heart and mind.

6 Facts Every Minister Should Remember About Reading

1. **Reading Will Often Discourage Unproductive Conversation With Others.** Have you ever sat beside someone who could not stop talking? Unfortunately, most people who love to talk a lot do not require anything significant to energize them. They will talk about anything just to avoid silence. When you keep a book handy, this usually discourages them.

2. **Keep A List Of The Books You Want To Read Each Month.** This prevents unwise selections in moments of boredom or fatigue. Every minister should read at least one book a week. At the beginning of each year, select fifty-two books that you would like to complete by the end of the year, and select a new one each Sunday. Just twenty pages a day will take you through a one hundred and forty page book every week.

3. **Bring Books With You On Airplane Trips And Vacations.** You are away from the busyness of your daily schedule. The phone cannot ring. The television is off. You can withdraw in your own private mental world. Focus *is* possible. You can purchase books in airports, but it is better for you to bring your own choice with you.

4. Keep Reading Material In Your Washroom. Avoid two-year-old magazines that do not keep you current and energized. Place books there that are a priority and important to you. I keep a Bible with my books as well.

5. Keep Two Books In Your Automobile At All Times. I suggest keeping a fiction book and a non-fiction book simultaneously. Moods vary. Sometimes, you want to *relax* and other times you will want to *learn.* Keep *both* convenient for such occasions. During traffic jams, this relieves the stress of "doing nothing" en route to an appointment.

6. Make Books Accessible To Others Riding With You As Well. This reading habit "brings your thoughts into captivity." This neutralizes the influence of others around you who would use these occasions to break your focus. *Your life stays on course.* Your focus is *protected.* You continue to grow even in the spare moments between appointments.

My life is quite full. There is little time for loneliness, self pity or "down time." Every moment matters to me. My hours matter to me. I travel a lot...I have for 40 years. I have noticed that the only time I want to read a novel is for relaxation on a plane. When I am home, I am emotionally attached to my projects and feeling the responsibility of over 50 staff members. So, I will take those moments on an airplane to nap (power naps), read the newspaper or read a novel. Sixteen years ago, I would write letters on planes and review business proposals. That has changed as well.

Your needs continuously change. Familiarize yourself with your personal rhythms. Cooperate with them and you can become more productive than you really realize.

Do not fight against the surges of energy in your life and ministry. Identify and flow with them. Make moments count.

Keep A Book With You At All Times.
It is One of the Secrets of the Uncommon Minister.

∾ 21 ∾

STOP BELITTLING YOUR PEOPLE FOR THEIR PURSUIT OF PROSPERITY

Financial Provision Is A Reward, Not A Curse.

God wants to bless His people. "No good thing will He withhold from them that walk uprightly," (Psalm 84:11).

I have heard some ministers publicly sneer at "prosperity preachers," and preach long messages on the snares of riches, while scores of their own people were desperate, without jobs, impoverished and bankrupt. *Only fools lecture on drowning during a drought.*

Late one night, I sat in a pastor's car. He was agitated. I had taught at length that night about our God of supernatural provision…the blessings that God wanted us to experience in our life. I addressed becoming debt-free, bringing the tithe to the Lord, and even putting your children through college. He had three basic fears.

3 Basic Fears Many Ministers Have About Receiving Offerings

1.   **Ministers Fear Criticism From The Wealthy Of Their Congregation.**

2.   **Ministers Are Often Unpersuaded Concerning The Harvest That God Promised His People For Giving.**

3.   **Ministers Often Believe It Is Improper To Emphasize Finances In A Spiritual Atmosphere.**

3 Answers To Your Fears In Receiving Offerings

1.   **The Wealthy Are Often Unconcerned About The**

Harvest Of The Poor. That is why Jesus declared, "The Spirit of the Lord is upon Me, because He hath anointed Me to preach the gospel to the poor," (Luke 4:18).

    2. **The Lord Of The Harvest Cannot Lie.** He will honor the Seeds of His people. "But this I say, He which soweth sparingly shall reap also sparingly; and he which soweth bountifully shall reap also bountifully," (2 Corinthians 9:6).

    3. **The Church Is The Most Appropriate Place On Earth For Faith In God To Be Unlocked For Finances.** Why permit your people to pursue financial blessing in an environment of money hungry, greedy, God-hating, God-ignoring hypocrites of the world system? Why can we not come into God's presence with great expectation that we will receive what we need from our Father's hand? (See Matthew 6:33.) Wisdom Key #49: *When You Let Go Of What Is In Your Hand, God Will Let Go Of What Is In His Hand.*

    I asked one minister five simple questions.

5 Questions I Wish Every Pastor Would Answer

    1.   "Do you have widows that cannot pay their apartment rent?" He did.

    2.   "Do you have people out of jobs?" He did.

    3.   "Have you made financial promises to missionaries that have been difficult to fulfill?" He had.

    4.   "Could you reach more souls with the Gospel in this city if you had more money for television and radio ministry?" He replied that it was the dream of his heart to reach his city.

    5.   "Who have *you* chosen as the Financial Mentor of your people?" That shocked him. He had made no plans at all for any Financial Mentor or Deliverer to come to his church and educate his people on budgets, debt and Seed faith.

    Yes, it is true, occasionally you will meet someone with more money than they will ever need or use. For them, the message on prosperity may seem unneeded, unheeded and unnecessary. This kind of logic would cause you to stop preaching salvation in the presence of believers!

    Please, please, stop discouraging your people from believing, expecting and receiving an Uncommon Provision from their Uncommon Provider.

▶ Their *future* depends on their *provision*.

▶ The future of your *church* depends on their *understanding* of sowing and reaping.

▶ The future of *souls* waiting to hear the Gospel depends on *their support* of the Gospel.

The Uncommon Minister will never discourage and weaken the desires of His people toward financial provision and prosperity.

Stop Belittling Your People For Their Pursuit Of Prosperity.

It is One of the Secrets of the Uncommon Minister.

RECOMMENDED INVESTMENTS:
Ten Lies Many People Believe About Money (Book/B-04/32 Pages/$5)
Seeds of Wisdom on Prosperity (Book/B-22/32 Pages/$5)
Greed, Gold and Giving (Book/B-66/32 Pages/$3)
31 Reasons People Do Not Receive Their Financial Harvest
 (6 Tapes/TS-38/$30)

Information
Births
Confidence.

-MIKE MURDOCK

≈ 22 ≈

SEE THE BIBLE AS THE SUCCESS HANDBOOK FOR YOUR MINISTRY

The Bible Is Your Success Handbook.

Once, while my father and I were in prayer, it occurred to me what I *would not know*, had the Bible *not* been given to me.

Without The Word...

1. **I Would Not Recognize The Weapons God Has Given Me For All Of My Battles With Satan.** I would not know anything about the weapon of praise, the weapon of singing, the weapon of intercession. I would not know that His Word is my greatest weapon. I would not know the effects of simply *resisting* satan.

2. **I Would Not Know Anything About The Fears Of My Enemy.** I would not even be aware that satan is afraid of me. (Read Matthew 4 and Luke 4: the temptations of Christ.)

3. **I Would Not Know Anything About The Angels Assigned To Assist Me.** I would be totally ignorant of the daily ministry of angels. "But to which of the angels said He at any time, Sit on My right hand, until I make thine enemies thy footstool? Are they not all ministering spirits, sent forth to minister for them who shall be heirs of salvation?" (Hebrews 1:13-14).

4. **I Would Be Ignorant Of The Holy Spirit Who Is Within Me And Beside Me.** I would have no knowledge at all of His power or how to *access His presence through singing.* "Make a joyful noise unto the Lord, all ye lands. Serve the Lord with gladness: come before His presence with singing," (Psalm 100:1-2).

"But the Comforter, which is the Holy Ghost, Whom the Father will send in My name, He shall teach you all things, and bring all things to your remembrance, whatsoever I have said unto you," (John 14:26).

"But ye shall receive power, after that the Holy Ghost is come upon you: and ye shall be witnesses unto Me both in Jerusalem, and in all Judaea, and in Samaria, and unto the uttermost part of the earth," (Acts 1:8).

Everything worth knowing comes through the Scriptures. Everything you need to know to succeed in your ministry is in The Word of God. "Blessed is the man that feareth the Lord, that delighteth greatly in His commandments. His Seed shall be mighty upon earth: the generation of the upright shall be blessed. Wealth and riches shall be in his house: and his righteousness endureth for ever," (Psalm 112:1-3).

5. I Would Not Know How To Judge The Behavior, The Conduct And The Words Of Other Men. I would be deceived a thousand times more if I did not have the Scriptures to judge other men's conduct and their words. "As it is written, There is none righteous, no, not one: There is none that understandeth, there is none that seeketh after God. They are all gone out of the way, they are together become unprofitable; there is none that doeth good, no, not one. Their throat is an open sepulchre; with their tongues they have used deceit; the poison of asps is under their lips: Whose mouth is full of cursing and bitterness: Their feet are swift to shed blood: Destruction and misery are in their ways: And the way of peace have they not known: There is no fear of God before their eyes," (Romans 3:10-18).

6. I Would Be Totally Ignorant Regarding The Reward System In The Scriptures. The Holy Spirit promised rewards for my obedience, for the battles that I win, for each labor of love. "And whosoever shall give to drink unto one of these little ones a cup of cold water only in the name of a disciple, verily I say unto you, he shall in no wise lose his reward," (Matthew 10:42). "If ye be willing and obedient, ye shall eat the good of the land," (Isaiah 1:19).

7. I Would Have No Knowledge Heaven Is An Ultimate Reward For Me If I Endure And Live A Holy Life. "In My Father's house are many mansions: if it were not so, I would have told you. I go to prepare a place for you," (John 14:2). "And ye shall be hated of all men for My name's sake: but he that endureth to the end shall be saved," (Matthew 10:22). "Not every one that saith unto Me, Lord, Lord, shall enter into the kingdom of heaven; but he that doeth the will of My Father which is in heaven," (Matthew 7:21). "Blessed is the man that endureth temptation: for when he is tried, he shall receive the crown of life, which the Lord hath promised to them that love Him," (James 1:12).

8.   I Would Have No Warning Of The Eternal Torment Of Hell Awaiting If I Refuse To Obey The Laws Of God. "And he cried and said, Father Abraham, have mercy on me, and send Lazarus, that he may dip the tip of his finger in water, and cool my tongue; for I am tormented in this flame," (Luke 16:24). "The Son of man shall send forth His angels, and they shall gather out of His kingdom all things that offend, and them which do iniquity; And shall cast them into a furnace of fire: there shall be wailing and gnashing of teeth," (Matthew 13:41-42).

9.   I Would Have No Motivation In Me To Withdraw From Evil And Abandon Myself To Righteousness. There is no *drawing* within, without The Word of God operating in me. "Thy Word have I hid in mine heart, that I might not sin against Thee," (Psalm 119:11).

Oh, think of the importance of The Word of God in your own life! No father would have any guidelines on raising his children! No mother would have standards by which to teach her children. *Embrace* The Holy Word of God with all your heart.

Believe it.

Listen to it on tape.

Memorize it daily.

Obey it.

Pray it aloud.

Preach it.

Study it.

See The Bible As The Success Handbook For Your Ministry.

It is One of the Secrets of the Uncommon Minister.

RECOMMENDED INVESTMENT:
The Book That Changed My Life (Book/B-117/32 Pages/$7)

What You Hear Decides How You Feel.

-MIKE MURDOCK

❦ 23 ❦

PREACH WHAT YOU WANT YOUR PEOPLE TO EXPERIENCE

Whatever You Preach Will Occur.

Billy Graham preaches salvation. What happens? Thousands make decisions to come to Christ and personally experience that salvation.

Richard Roberts preaches on The Healing Jesus. What occurs under his ministry? Thousands receive the healing touch of Jesus of Nazareth.

▶ Whatever you *teach* your people will become the *experience* of their life.

▶ What they *hear* determines what they *pursue.*

▶ What they *pursue* will determine what they *experience.*

If you refuse to minister the healing power of Jesus, disease, sickness and pain will flourish among your people.

Any Uncontested Enemy Succeeds.

Dr. Fredrick K. C. Price wrote an excellent book, "Practical Suggestions for Successful Ministry." On page 19, concerning past years he says, "The reason why no one ever received healing was because no one ever preached the Word on Divine healing."

If you refuse to teach the principles of financial blessing to your people, debt and poverty will flourish. Anger and resentment will seep under the surface in every home.

▶ *An Unexposed Enemy Will Master Many People.*

▶ *An Unconfronted Enemy Is An Accepted Enemy.*

It is *your* responsibility to set captives free.

You are their *Deliverer.*

You see their enemy.

You must *expose* their enemy.

You must *confront* their enemy.

Teach your people how to overcome that enemy.

3 Messages Every Minister Should Preach

1.   **When You Preach Supernatural Love, Hatred Will Die.** Caring, compassion and love will become the qualities of the people who hear your Seeds of Wisdom on the love of God.

2.   **When You Preach The Wrath Of God, The Fear Of God Will Be Birthed In Your People.** That fear of God will become the beginning of their Wisdom. Their hatred for evil will grow.

3.   **When You Preach On The Return Of Christ, A Godly Hope Will Rise In The Hearts Of Every Family.** The signs of the time will become more meaningful to them. "Beloved, now are we the sons of God, and it doth not yet appear what we shall be: but we know that, when He shall appear, we shall be like Him; for we shall see Him as He is. And every man that hath this hope in Him purifieth himself, even as He is pure," (1 John 3:2-3).

None of us knows everything.

Remember *every* minister is ignorant in some area. That is why God created so many of us. The body of Christ can be ministered to effectively through the variation of callings and anointings. This is common among doctors. The ear doctor may be next door to a throat doctor. The pianist is not necessarily effective on the drums. Both are musicians, with different gifts.

Follow The Example Of Successful Pastors Who Invite Other Ministries Whose Focus Differs From Their Own. One minister friend of mine feels inadequate to teach on financial prosperity. He calls in other teaching ministries who present the message effectively to his people. Another pastor friend of mine said, "I simply do not understand how Bible prophecy links up with today's events. My church responsibilities at the hospitals, counseling and overseeing the business transactions have robbed me of the time needed to develop my Wisdom in the area of Bible prophecy. So, twice a year, I bring in other ministries for one week to teach every night and day that part of the Gospel to my people."

This is Wisdom.

Whatever You Lack Is Hidden In Someone Else Near You. Drop your pail in their well!

Value The Focus Of Other Ministries Around You. You see, the man who preaches soul-winning may lack Wisdom on the Return of Christ. His focus is soul-winning. Treasure his calling. Another minister, whose focus is prayer and fasting may not understand the Laws of Financial Prosperity. Yet, he loves the presence of God and moves freely and comfortably in the areas of receiving answers to prayer. Honor his focus.

Preach What You Want Your People To Experience.

It is One of the Secrets of the Uncommon Minister.

The Proof
Of Passion
Is Pursuit.

-MIKE MURDOCK

⮞ 24 ⮜

KNOW YOUR SHEEP

Your Sheep Are Worth Knowing.

Jesus commanded Peter, "Feed My sheep," (see John 21:16). This verse is pregnant with Wisdom.

Jesus *loved* people.

Jesus *sought out* the lonely, *encouraged* the downcast and *corrected* the wayward.

Jesus wanted His disciples to value, cherish and treasure the opportunity to love the lost and feed His sheep.

6 Things Every Minister Should Know About The Sheep

1.   Know Their Assignment. Your people have incredible qualities. Patience? Kindness? Some are going through the most difficult trials of their life. Yet, they keep a sweet spirit.

As you look across the audience, you are looking into the face of overcomers, fighters and victors.

How *important* are they to you?

Are they simply *numbers?*

Do you ever call their names before the Lord?

Are you aware of their *Assignment?*

2.   Know Their Dominant Gifts, Skills And Strengths. The Holy Spirit planted uncommon talents within them. Do you know what those gifts really are? Do you know what each person in your congregation does *daily?* Certainly, when your church is enormous, attended by thousands, that is impossible to some degree. However, your *concern* should exist. Your caring should be *obvious*.

3.   Know Their Background.   You see, the pain we experienced in our childhood often affects the *decisions* we make, the *offenses* we collect and the fears that are birthed.

Never preach to the needs you do not feel.

4.   Know Their Weaknesses. Jesus said, "Simon, behold, Satan hath desired to have you, that he may sift you as wheat: But I have prayed for thee," (Luke 22:31-32).

Peter heard this.

Peter felt loved.

Peter knew Jesus interceded for him daily.

How can you pray *effectively* for those whose weaknesses you have not yet discovered?

5.   Know Their Passion And Obsession. You see, your people will invest time, energy and finances into their obsession and passion. Jesus did this. He showed up on the shores of Galilee. He even interrogated His disciples, "Have ye any meat?" (John 21:5). He wanted to know about their fishing success. True interest is so rare.

Genuine concern is the greatest gift you can give. It always begins a miracle relationship.

6.   Know Their Struggles. You are busy, as a minister of the Gospel, supervising many projects, staff members and situations. Yet, your people are hurting. That young couple in the back of the sanctuary may be battling to pay the rent on their apartment.

The single mother is struggling against anger and hate because her ex-husband refuses to provide her any child support.

The teenagers on the back row feel unwanted and unloved. They are struggling for a sense of significance and worth.

Do *you* remember that?

Do you *feel* that?

Are you *changing that?*

The words of Jesus ring clear, "My sheep hear My voice, and I know them, and they follow Me," (John 10:27). Why? He had invested time and attention in the relationship. "Know them which labour among you," (1 Thessalonians 5:12).

4 Powerful Ways To Increase Your Personal Knowledge Of Your People

1.   Have Your People Fill Out Questionnaires, Send You Pictures Of Their Business And Describe Their Greatest

Needs.

2. **Keep A Prayer Book In Your Secret Place With The Photographs And Desires Of Your People And Their Families.**

3. **Train Qualified Spiritual Leaders For Different Groups In Your Church Who Will Know Them.**

4. **Schedule A Variety Of Meetings, Events And Celebrations.** Some have special concerts for youth, birthday parties and graduation celebrations. Why? Just to *know* your people.

Jesus knows you. That is the reason for your loyalty to Him. *Know Your Sheep.*

It is One of the Secrets of the Uncommon Minister.

RECOMMENDED INVESTMENTS:
Seeds of Wisdom on Relationships, Volume 2 (Book/B-14/32 Pages/$3)
The Wisdom Commentary, Volume 2 (Book/B-220PB/312 Pages/$25)
The School of Wisdom #6: The Twelve Priorities of Life (6 Tapes/TS-54/$30)
12 Proofs of Love (CD/WCPL-10/$10)

Tired Eyes Rarely See
A Great Future.

-MIKE MURDOCK

❧ 25 ❧

NEVER MAKE IMPORTANT MINISTRY DECISIONS WHEN YOU ARE TIRED

Tired Eyes Rarely See A Great Future.

When you are weary, you cannot discern accurately.

You do not have the same kind of faith, the same kind of enthusiasm or the same kind of patience.

When you are rested, you are strengthened.

8 Mistakes Fatigue Produces

1. **When You Are Tired, Mountains Look Bigger.** When you are tired at night, things that normally would appear simple suddenly seem burdensome and very complex to you. Tasks that really require a minimal effort suddenly seem too much to take on.

2. **When You Are Tired, Valleys Seem Deeper.** Discouraging factors seem to enlarge. Disappointment seems keener and stronger when your body is fatigued.

3. **When You Are Tired, Offenses Come Easier.** It has happened in my own life. I seem more offended than I normally would be. *Little things* become big in my mind.

When I am tired, I often replay in my mind wrongs that people have done to me.

When I am rested, my mind moves to positive, wonderful and glorious dreams, things I want to accomplish and do.

Fatigue affects me in the opposite manner. I begin to meditate on my own mistakes and the mistakes of others. There is a Scripture that indicates that satan wants to wear out the saints. I believe it. "And he shall speak great words against the most High, and shall wear out the saints of the most High, and think to change times and laws: and they shall be given into his hand until a time and times and the dividing of time," (Daniel 7:25).

Jesus understood this. That is why He encouraged His disciples to "come ye apart and rest awhile." Or, as Vance Havner suggested, "Ye will come apart!" (See Mark 6:31.)

One of the great presidents of the United States once said that he would never make a decision past 3:00 in the afternoon. His mind was too tired and weary to consider every option available.

4.   When You Are Tired, You Become Less Tolerant Of The Views Of Others. When others are weary, they seem less understanding of your own opinions and views as well.

5.   When You Are Tired, Your Focus Turns To What You Want Instead Of The Appropriate Method For Achieving It.

6.   When You Are Tired, Your Focus Will Usually Turn To A Short-Term Goal Rather Than Your Long-Term Goals.

7.   When You Are Tired, Your Words Will Become Rash, Inappropriate And Even Harsh Towards Those Who Truly Love You.

8.   When You Are Tired, You Become Unwilling To Invest The Appropriate And Sufficient Time In Planning Ahead On Projects.

Rest *restores* you.

Rest *energizes* you.

Rest improves the quality of decision-making.

Never Make Important Ministry Decisions When You Are Tired.

It is One of the Secrets of the Uncommon Minister.

～ 26 ～

RESPECT THE SCHEDULE, FOCUS AND NEEDS OF YOUR PEOPLE

Respect The Responsibilities Of Your People.

I had finished a two-day school of The Holy Spirit up north. It had been a glorious two days. The presence of God was so powerful. I loved being with my friends and partners, as always.

Due to the airline schedule, I had to leave thirty minutes earlier than planned. Another minister was going to conclude the session for me. Due to the airline schedule, two flights were necessary, and would allow me to arrive at my destination at 1:00 a.m.

My schedule was tight. In fact, I would barely arrive on time at the church where I was scheduled. So, I announced to everyone present that my plane schedule was too close for me to stay afterwards for additional conversation.

Yet, as I was rushing toward the door with my briefcase, my associate by my side, five to seven people stopped me. Standing in front of me, they *insisted* that I autograph my books they had purchased. Some insisted that I hear about an experience that had occurred in their life.

Each one of them had *totally ignored my schedule,* my words, and showed little caring whatsoever.

Did they love me? Not really.

They loved *themselves.*

Their only obsession was *to get something* they wanted, regardless of the toll it took on me.

My needs meant little to them. My schedule was unimportant to them.

The Holy Spirit is always offended by such insensitivity and lack of caring for others.

3 Keys In Respecting Time

1.   Always Make Sure Your Time With Someone Is Appropriate For Their Schedule. Do not use intimidating language or statements. One that I often hear is, "Do you have any time for *me?*" This is simply an attempt to intimidate me. Or, statements like, "You *never* have time for me. You *always* have time for *everyone else!*"

This is *victim* vocabulary. This kind of person has no true regard for others. They are obsessed with themselves. You can never give them enough time and attention to satisfy them.

2.   Always Mark Those Who Show Disregard And Disrespect For Your Time...The Most Precious Gift God Gave You. One pastor here in Dallas refuses any personal counseling to newcomers. They must qualify for private counseling by attending six continuous weeks of his teaching services. *Those who abuse your time will misuse your Wisdom.*

3.   Honor The Work Schedule And Unique Family Needs Of Your People. As an evangelist, it has taken years to understand this key. Since I come to a church only once a year, I always expect everyone to drop everything they are doing to attend my special conference! Sometimes, people have to rush out because of their jobs and other responsibilities.

One night, I was startled to see a man leave as I was speaking. In my brashness, I publicly questioned him rather jokingly.

"Are you angry at my ministry?" I asked.

He looked back so embarrassed as everyone stared at him.

"I am late for my work shift tonight," he replied quietly.

I was embarrassed beyond words. I could have crawled under the front seat. I simply had not understood *his* schedule.

Successful ministers recognize that many mothers have restless children; many fathers work long hours. They honor and respect this, and their people appreciate this respect.

Respect The Schedule, Focus And Needs Of Your People.

It is One of the Secrets of the Uncommon Minister.

⇝ 27 ⇝

ANTICIPATE AND AVOID THE TRAP OF UNANSWERABLE QUESTIONS

Satan Asked The First Question.

Accept the fact: you are not God. That is why the apostle Paul wrote to his protégé, "But foolish and unlearned questions avoid, knowing that they do gender strifes," (2 Timothy 2:23).

I have a tenacious curiosity. My mind is in constant pursuit of answers and solutions. There is nothing really wrong with desiring truthful answers. Everyone knows that.

However, it was a *simple question* in the beautiful and gorgeous Garden of Eden, *that birthed the greatest tragedy* that has ever occurred in the history of man.

7 Things To Remember About Questions

1.   **Satan Asked The First Question On Record.** "Now the serpent was more subtil than any beast of the field which the Lord God had made. And he said unto the woman, Yea, hath God said, Ye shall not eat of every tree of the garden?" (Genesis 3:1).

He set the trap.

Doubt was the bait.

Eve fell for it.

Adam followed.

You and I have paid a dear price for this tragic mistake.

2.   **Ask The Questions God Likes To Answer.**

The obedient ask, *"What* must I do?"

The disobedient ask, *"Why* should I do it?"

3.   **Discern Questions Nobody Is Qualified To Answer.** I remember sitting around a table asking stupid questions such as,

"Which came first, the chicken or the egg?" In my early ministry, I remember sitting on a Greyhound bus trying to answer a question from a cynical old man, "Who did Cain marry?" What a waste of time!

4.   Laugh At The Attempts Of Cynics To Intimidate You With Difficult Questions. Do not get angry. You see, the cynic is not living the answers he *already* knows in his heart. He is using questions *as a smoke screen* to distract you from his own rebellion. The Pharisees tried this. Jesus moved *away* from them and went home with Zacchaeus who recognized his need of Jesus.

5.   Stop Trying To Answer *Unanswerable* Questions About Divine Healing. One of the greatest and most effective men in our generation is Oral Roberts. He once said, "I cannot figure out healing. I pray for some, I do not think will be healed, and God heals them. I pray for others, I just know will be healed, and they do not receive it. *It is all still a mystery to me.*" He does not *play* God.

6.   Do Not Try To Explain Tragedies. Nobody can fully explain why someone is healed and another dies. My own parents cannot explain the death of two of their children. Yet, they have embraced the goodness of God and the "evilness" of satan. God gives life, and satan takes life. (See John 10:10.) Thousands leave the Highway of Answers to build their entire conversation around the Pothole of Questions.

7.   You Cannot Climb Mountains Studying Pebbles. Often, after delivering powerful Wisdom Keys on Success, I have been approached by someone who ignored everything I taught that night. They had searched for one possible question that would "stump me." In my beginning years, I thought they were sincere. I wasted hundreds of hours trying to become "The Answer Man" to everybody. It was ridiculous!

What To Do When Someone Asks You An Unanswerable Question

1.   Invite Them To Pray With You For The Spirit Of Wisdom To Reveal Answers.

2.   Recommend An Appropriate Book Or Specific Scriptures That Are Helpful.

3.   Invite Them To Invest In A Tape Of Your Ministry That Could Revolutionize Their Life.

Their response to your three suggestions reveals the depth of their true appetite for Wisdom.

Time-wasters are everywhere. I meet them daily. Time is the most precious gift I have, and I refuse to permit a cynic or a fool to destroy it.

Avoid The Trap Of Unanswerable Questions.

It is One of the Secrets of the Uncommon Minister.

You Can Create
With Your Seed
What You Cannot Buy
With Your Money.

-MIKE MURDOCK

~28~

STOP HURRYING YOUR OFFERINGS

Good Things Take Time.

The mentorship of Jesus required 30 years. The training of Moses required 80 years. "The Lord is good unto them that wait for Him," (Lamentations 3:25).

I am appalled at the disrespect shown toward Offerings.

The Holy Spirit is *grieved* over disrespect toward Offerings.

► The Offering is a Love Moment with God.

► The Offering is the Golden Door to Harvest.

► The Offering is the Season for Thanksgiving and Worship.

The Uncommon Minister knows this and gives quality time to the celebration of the Tithes and Offerings to our Heavenly Father, the Uncommon Provider.

Fewer than twenty times in my life have I attended any service where I have had sufficient time to secure my checkbook and write a check before the usher appeared by my side.

3 Important Keys About The Moment Of Thanksgiving

1.   It Takes Time For The Focus Of People To Change From Watching An Interesting Choir To Understanding The Value Of Their Seed. Your church members have lived in a climate of doubt for seven days, 168 hours of fear and unbelief. The television news has made them scared and fearful of the volatile changes facing the banks. Unexpected bills have arrived in the mail. The roof suddenly leaks. The car breaks down. An expected promotion becomes a disappointment. Now, your church member sits there on Sunday morning with his head whirling with thoughts and questions such as, "How will I squeeze a new alternator into my budget? Where will I get the money to put my son through college? How will we get the second car that we desperately need?"

Suddenly, the minister appears and makes a statement in the midst of this volcanic eruption of doubts and financial fears and says, "Will the ushers come forward as we receive the morning Tithes and Offerings?"

Disengaging from these thoughts of debt, credit cards and impending bills...is a miracle within itself.

2. Your People Deserve Quality Time To Hear From Your Burning Heart What You Know About Their Promised Harvest. They are facing a mountain of bills. Their mind is in torment because their mate made an unexpected and unwise purchase. Their car repair bill was horrendous...and you are suddenly rushing them to bring their tithe and offerings to God?

Talk to them.

Talk to their *heart*.

Address their *hopes.*

Remove their doubts.

The Word of God *will* work for them.

Focus their attention on the Lord of the Harvest, the God who will *not* fail them.

3. Impregnate Their Seeds With A Vision... A Portrait Of The Promise Of Uncommon Provision. Elijah did this when he approached the widow of Zarephath. (Read 1 Kings 17.) Paint an accurate picture of Hope for them.

That is what the Offering is about.

The Offering is not to pay for the new roof of the sanctuary, to buy an extra ten acres of ground next door or to pay your salary.

The Seeds of your people are pregnant with their future.

Make the moment *count.*

Make it a *Great* Moment.

Make it a *Hopeful* Moment.

Make it a *Mentorship* Moment.

Make it a *Love* Moment.

Make it a *Faith* Moment.

Make it a *Miracle* Moment.

Make Every Offering The Birthplace For Harvest.

Those who really love food do not want to be rushed through this moment of pleasure in their day.

Those who enjoy loving their mate consider it an investment worthy of complete attention.

Do not rush through the most important moment of every service...the Moment of Thanksgiving, Respect and Honoring of our Uncommon Provider...our Jehovah-Jireh.

The Uncommon Minister refuses to rush through the Offering that will forever change the future of his people, his vision and his ministry.

Stop Hurrying Your Offerings.

It is One of the Secrets of the Uncommon Minister.

RECOMMENDED INVESTMENTS:
Seeds of Wisdom on Seed-Faith, Volume 4 (Book/B-16/32 Pages/$3)
31 Reasons People Do Not Receive Their Financial Harvest
  (6 Tapes/TS-38/$30)

You Will Only
Be Remembered
For Your Obsession.

-MIKE MURDOCK

✒ 29 ✒

MASTER ONE TOPIC IN THE BIBLE

━━━━━━━━━━━━━►❖◄━━━━

Know One Subject More Than Anyone Else.

When I was 15 years old, an extraordinary minister came to my father's church. He was articulate, brilliant and persuasive. He took a special interest in me, and I responded.

"No man has the right to call himself a man of God who reads less than twenty chapters a day in the Scriptures," he declared. "Read the Scriptures daily, continuously. *Become an authority on at least one topic in the Bible.*"

I believed him. So, at the tender age of fifteen, I began to read the Bible consistently, a minimum of twenty chapters a day. Later, I began reading forty chapters a day which helped me read the Bible completely through every thirty days. Some would criticize this method of reading a lot of Scripture thinking you could not retain very much. However, I discovered reading the Scriptures continuously brought an increased awareness of the passion of God, a relationship with His people. Rather than simply read three or four chapters a day that would "keep the conscience okay," I really wanted to have a general working knowledge of Scripture.

As I matured, I focused on one topic at a time. Now, I have discovered that your knowledge can soar quickly when you develop a passion and focus. Suppose you wanted to know everything in Scripture about *"Faith."* That is a marvelous subject. In fact, without *faith* you cannot even please or pleasure God. God has a desperate desire to be believed.

10 Helpful Thoughts On Mastering One Topic In Scripture

Let's imagine your focus to master is...*Faith.*

1.   **Read Through The Bible And Circle In Red (Or Highlight In Pink) Every Scripture Relating To That Topic Of Faith.** When you open your Bible, you will immediately see every Scripture connected to your focus, *Faith*. Mark those Scriptures that reveal the benefits and blessings of *using* your Faith. This will include *examples* such as Joshua and Caleb in the Old Testament. Highlight Scriptures that show the consequences of *not* using your *Faith*. Your goal is to become an authority on *Faith*.

2.   **Create A Yearly Calendar Of 365 Favorite Scriptures On *Faith*.** Begin a memorization program of one Scripture each day...your passion, *Faith*. It is important to tie together the focus of your life, *Faith*, with your daily living and circumstances. This calendar is a legacy for your family. Discuss your Scripture-of-the-Day on *Faith* at the breakfast table. Place it on your refrigerator door. Pin it on the bulletin board. I promise you, if you memorize 365 Scriptures on *Faith*, you will become the expert on the topic of *Faith* in *any* conversation!

3.   **Collect Books And Tapes From Teachers Who Teach On Faith.** You will be amazed how The Holy Spirit supernaturally guides your life into uncommon relationships with mentors to teach you.

4.   **Keep A List Of Questions Regarding Faith.** This enables you to benefit from any moment you are in the presence of someone else who is an authority on *Faith*.

5.   **Conclude Every Telephone Conversation With A Special Prayer For Your Friend That God Will "Increase Your Faith."**

6.   **Listen To The Bible Daily On Cassette Tape.** It increases your Faith. "So then faith cometh by hearing, and hearing by the word of God," (Romans 10:17).

7.   **Pray For Increased Understanding And Revelation Concerning Faith.** As you get alone with The Holy Spirit in The Secret Place, He will open your eyes of understanding. "Ask, and it shall be given you; seek, and ye shall find; knock, and it shall be opened unto you: For every one that asketh receiveth; and he that seeketh findeth; and to him that knocketh it shall be opened," (Matthew 7:7-8).

8.   **Set Aside A Specific Time Every Day To Read A Book**

On Faith. Be militant and decisive about this appointment with Wisdom.

9. Become Known For Your Obsession To Understand Faith. When someone mentions Thomas Edison, everyone thinks about inventions. When someone mentions the Wright Brothers, everyone thinks of airplanes. It should be this way with you. Everyone should know your passion is—*Faith*. Open every church service quoting a verse concerning *Faith*.

10. Maintain Your Wisdom Notebook On Faith. Write down every thought, idea and even poems on Faith. You will be thrilled to see your progress in the coming twelve months. Your life and ministry should become remembered by this focus.

Whatever topic The Holy Spirit leads you toward, give it your total focus.

It will change your ministry forever.

4 Benefits Emerge When You Become An Expert On One Topic

1. Your Confidence Toward God Will Multiply. His Word throbs with strength, energy and joy. Every word He speaks will breathe a new energy into your ministry unparalleled by anything else you do.

2. Your Confidence Toward Your Own Dreams And Goals Will Increase. Knowledge makes you comfortable. Knowledge increases your confidence about everything you do.

3. Others Will Receive Your Ministry With Increased Confidence. As your people listen to The Word of God pouring from your lips, they will become excited about your ability to help them and increase their knowledge of God.

4. Your Knowledge Of Other Subjects Will Instantly Increase. For example, when you study *angels,* you will discover Lucifer and demon spirits, ex-angels dethroned by God. When you study *faith,* you will learn so much about prayer, The Secret Place and the intercession ministry of Jesus. When you study The Holy Spirit, you will fall in love with Jesus more than ever.

Master One Topic In The Bible.

It is One of the Secrets of the Uncommon Minister.

Those Pursuing Greatness Are Worthy Of Pursuit.

-MIKE MURDOCK

⤳ 30 ⤳

TREASURE THE CALL TO PREACH THAT IS ON YOUR LIFE

You Are More Than A Spiritual Administrator.
You are more than the CEO of a church.
You are more than a counselor.
Your Assignment from God is to preach.
Preach until chains fall off captives present.
Preach until disease is destroyed.
Preach until the power of God falls.

Paul embraced his calling to preach, "Whereunto I am appointed a preacher, and an apostle, and a teacher of the Gentiles," (2 Timothy 1:11).

11 Facts About Preaching

1. **Preaching Is How God Manifests His Word.** "But hath in due times manifested His word through preaching, which is committed unto me," (Titus 1:3).

2. **Preaching Persuades.** "Holding fast the faithful Word as he hath been taught, that he may be able by sound doctrine both to exhort and to convince the gainsayers," (Titus 1:9).

3. **Preaching Protects Men From The Judgments And Wrath Of A Holy God.** "Knowing therefore the terror of the Lord, we persuade men," (2 Corinthians 5:11).

4. **Preaching Is The Powerful Weapon That Saves People From Eternal Damnation.** "For the preaching of the cross is to them that perish foolishness; but unto us which are saved it is the power of God," (1 Corinthians 1:18).

5. **Preach The Gospel Rather Than Your Personal Prejudices And Opinions.** "For Christ sent me not to baptize, but to preach the gospel: not with wisdom of words, less the cross of

Christ should be made of none effect," (1 Corinthians 1:17).

6.   Separate Yourself From Anything That Weakens The Effectiveness Of Your Preaching. "Paul, a servant of Jesus Christ, called to be an apostle, separated unto the gospel of God," (Romans 1:1).

7.   Preach Because You Are Accountable To God For The Souls Of Men And Women. "Let a man so account of us, as of the ministers of Christ, and stewards of the mysteries of God. Moreover it is required in stewards, that a man be found faithful...but He that judgeth me is the Lord," (1 Corinthians 4:1-2, 4).

8.   Preaching Births Spiritual Sons And Daughters Under Your Anointing Who Will Carry On The Message After Your Passing. "I write not these things to shame you, but as my beloved sons I warn you. For though ye have ten thousand instructors in Christ, yet have ye not many fathers: for in Christ Jesus I have begotten you through the gospel," (1 Corinthians 4:14-15).

9.   Preaching Inspires Others To Follow Your Pattern In Life. The apostle Paul understood this. "Wherefore I beseech you, be ye followers of me,"   (1 Corinthians 4:16).

10.   Preach More Strongly To Those Who Are Mature Enough To Receive It. The apostle Paul did. "But strong meat belongeth to them that are of full age, even those who by reason of use have their senses exercised to discern both good and evil," (Hebrews 5:14).

11.   Preach With Gratitude Because You Have Been Chosen By God Himself To Preach This Gospel. The apostle Paul lived thankful. "But the Lord said unto him, Go thy way: for he is a chosen vessel unto Me, to bear My name before the Gentiles, and kings, and the children of Israel," (Acts 9:15).

Treasure The Call To Preach.

It is One of the Secrets of the Uncommon Minister.

RECOMMENDED INVESTMENT:
The School of Wisdom #3: What I'd Do Differently If I Could Live My Life
   Over Again (6 Tapes/TS-43/$30)

⟡ 31 ⟡

KNOW YOURSELF

Study Yourself.

Know your greatest strength. One of my favorite people shared an interesting illustration a few days ago when I spoke for her conference in Denver, Colorado. She had visited China. Admiring their World Class ping pong team, she asked the teachers how they corrected the weaknesses of their players. The reply came, "We ignore the weaknesses and focus on developing their strengths. Their strengths will override those weaknesses." This is a Secret of Uncommon Champions.

Do not waste your entire ministry grieving over your weaknesses or failures.

4 Helpful Keys In Studying Yourself

1. Find Your Dominant Strength. Is it compassion for people? Is it long and enduring patience? Is it uncommon energy and enthusiasm? Is it the ability to be loyal in the face of adversity? Is it exceptional skill at management and administration? Is your speaking powerful, expressive or magnetic? Do you have the ability to *motivate* a small team around you? Is your greatest gift to hire uncommon staff? Your greatest strength is the Golden Gate to an *Uncommon* Ministry.

2. Know Your Greatest Weakness. Jesus knew the weakness of Peter, "Satan hath desired to have you, that he may sift you as wheat: But I have prayed for thee, that thy faith fail not," (Luke 22:31-32).

I will never forget the shocking statement made by a famous and well-known pastor of our day. "My greatest weakness is women. Some men have a weakness for drugs, alcohol or gambling. I love beautiful women. So, I refuse to permit myself to be alone when I travel. I keep two businessmen with me every hour of the day." That seems absurd to a young novice in the ministry who believes that the power of God conquers all. However, the Uncommon Man of God refuses to "give place to the devil," (see Ephesians 4:27). He moves *away* from the temptation zone, not *toward* it.

3.   Know Your Greatest Fear. Everything you do is moving you toward something you truly desire or moving you toward something you fear. *Your fears are determining the kinds of decisions you make.*

Yesterday, a young man sat in the Wisdom Room of my home. He is a very effective and skilled young pastor from a distant city and state. He asked my counsel regarding a loan of almost two million dollars.

"Run from debt," I implored. "Give God time to produce a financial miracle. You see, debt will wipe the smile off your face. Debt changes the kinds of decisions you make. Debt will become your obsession, and you will lose the spontaneity and joy of your incredible ministry. Do not put your small congregation under that huge indebtedness. They will feel differently toward you than they do today. You will not feel the change during the first six or twelve months. However, the time will come when you will dread seeing that twenty year note every day."

After he left, several truths dawned. Apparently, he has no memories of really painful financial losses. He was new at pastoring. He saw only victories and joys ahead. I was speaking from my own past pain, fears and torments. I hate poverty. I hate debt. I hate pain. I despise walking into a bank and having them respond to me like I have leprosy.

4.   Know Your Own Needs. I need times of *solitude.* I need *changes.* I require great freedom of movement in my life. I love *order* around me. I enjoy candles, waterfalls and water fountains. Climate matters to me. Because I recognize my needs, I can create the appropriate environment which unlocks my creativity and accommodates my needs.

Twenty years ago, I did not discern my own needs. Following a divorce, someone asked me, "What kind of furniture do you like?" I had no idea.

"Where would you like to live?" I had never thought about it.

"What is your greatest goal of your life?" I could not really define it.

What do you need to keep *spiritually* motivated? What do you need and require from your closest friends? What do you require from your staff? What do you need financially to live the lifestyle you really enjoy?

I am amused at friends who think I should "go hunting." I love animals. I have numerous animals and cannot imagine myself killing animals. You see, that is something my friends love to do.

Others insist that I "golf." I attempted it twice. For the life of me, I cannot imagine hitting a ball far away from me, going to where the ball landed and hitting it *further* away! Those who enjoy golf mystify me. It certainly is not exercise. Nobody walks fast. In fact, they use little golf carts! *Whatever.* Their needs are simply different than my own.

Know Yourself.

It is One of the Secrets of the Uncommon Minister.

Give Someone What
They Cannot Find
Anywhere Else And They
Will Keep Returning.

-MIKE MURDOCK

∽ 32 ∽

ALWAYS ALLOW OTHERS ROOM TO TURN AROUND

Everybody Makes Mistakes.

Everybody deserves the chance to change. Permit them to do so.

When pressure increases, those around us are often affected. Their stress then influences us. The incessant, constant demands of others often birth impatience...and mistakes. During these moments, *your mercy is necessary.*

Wrong words are often blurted out. Inaccurate assessments are made. Wrong decisions occur. Think back upon your own ministry. Many factors drove you to moments of indiscretion, cutting words and angry outburst. You have made mistakes also.

6 Steps In Allowing Others The Opportunity To Change

1. **Permit Forgiveness.** *Do not force others to live by bad decisions in their past.* What you sow will come back to you a hundred times. Give them space to re-enter the relationship *with dignity.* "Blessed are the merciful, for they shall obtain mercy," (Matthew 5:7).

2. **Forgive 490 Times.** "Then came Peter to Him, and said, Lord, how oft shall my brother sin against me, and I forgive him? till seven times? Jesus saith unto him, I say not unto thee, Until seven times: but, Until seventy times seven," (Matthew 18:21-22). Forgive seventy times seven.

3. **Give Them Enough Time.** Things are happening which you cannot see. Sometimes it takes weeks for a person to change. Give them a Season of *Silence.*

4. **Give Them An Open Door For Expression...A Chance**

To Explain Themselves. They may *not* have the right words the *first time.* Be willing to *listen longer.*

5. **Give Them Time To Evaluate Every Part Of The Puzzle.** You are looking at one part. They are considering many things they have yet to discuss with you.

6. **Give Them Time To Discover The Truth About You.** You already know you. They do not. They do not know all of your *flaws.* They do not know all of your *capabilities.* They do not understand your *memories.* Your pain. Your goals or dreams.

Mercy Is The Seed For Longevity...in Love, Marriage, Relationships and the Ministry.

Always Allow Others Room To Turn Around.

It is One of the Secrets of the Uncommon Minister.

∾ 33 ∾

TASTE YOUR PRESENT; IT HAS TAKEN YOU A LIFETIME TO GET HERE

Moments Should Be Tasted.

Your day should be *savored,* not gulped down.

Your life is a special and glorious gift from your Creator. Do not rush through it. Stop long enough to drink deep from each day. View each day as a wonderful fountain. Stop. Stand still. Take a deep drink from the sweet waters of the *Present.* You see, *Today* is really the only place you will ever exist. When you arrive in your future, you will *rename it...Today.*

Yesterday is in the *tomb.*

Tomorrow is in the *womb.*

If you do not know how to enjoy the Today that exists, you probably will enjoy few days in your future.

7 Keys To The Unhurried Lifestyle

1. **Happiness Is A "Now" Place.** It is not a future destination or place of arrival. "This is the day which the Lord hath made; we will rejoice and be glad in it," (Psalm 118:24).

2. **Savor This Moment Because The Future Is Not Guaranteed.** "Whereas ye know not what shall be on the morrow. For what is your life? It is even a vapour, that appeareth for a little time, and then vanisheth away," (James 4:14).

3. **Over-Scheduling Is Death, To A Joyful Ministry.** *Do not over-schedule today.* *Reschedule* tasks you can do with more excellence tomorrow.

Raise your present turf to its highest level of excellence.

4. **Insist That Every Moment Be A Moment Of**

Excellence. Whatever you do, do with all your heart. *Conversations* should be conducted at the highest level. *Exercise* should be done properly. Planning should be thorough, not hurried.

    5.   **Hurried Lives Are Not Necessarily Productive Lives.** Busyness is not always a forward movement. Activity is not necessarily progressive. I have been around people who "flurry." Their emotional energy is higher than anyone around them. Yet, nothing truly significant occurs.

    6.   **Calm And Gentle People Are Not Necessarily Unproductive.** Some of the most extraordinary and uncommon achievers appear to be methodical, unhurried and thoughtful. Their *decisions* are significant. Their instructions are *clear* and defined. Precision marks every step.

    7.   **Progress Is The Result Of Genuine Enthusiasm, Not Unfocused Energy.** Remember the playground? Laughter, energy and enthusiasm abounded. Thirty minutes later, everybody was tired, worn out or wanted to "do something else."

    My own life is quite busy. Let me give you an example. Yesterday, I finished a conference in Virginia and took a plane to Pittsburgh. Then, I changed planes to fly to Ohio. I dictated two chapters for a new book, reviewed twenty to thirty pages of faxes, wrote letters and telephoned seven pastors and friends. Then, I spoke at a special banquet for a church where $200,000 was committed to a new house of the Lord. The pastor met me this morning, drove me to the airport where I continued to dictate en route. I *read* on the plane, *dozed* a bit, and came straight to the hotel upon arrival.

    Yet, I was not in a frenzy.

    Let me explain. When I arrived today, in my beautiful suite in Tampa, Florida, I took my cassette recorder out of my briefcase. Praise music filled this beautiful hotel suite. I began to praise and worship and thank God for the wonderful life He has given me. Then, I called room service to bring my dinner meal early. Service will begin in three hours. While waiting for my meal, I went downstairs to receive a special package containing my new book from my printer. I unpacked my luggage, and within moments, my meal had arrived. You can create a marvelous atmosphere…even in a hotel room. No, I am not lonely. The Holy Spirit is with me. He is my *focus*… my life and my joy. Millions are attempting to fill their lives with activities, new friends and "things."

I refuse to race through life.

I will walk through the Garden of Life...I will not run. I will smell the fragrance of His presence, drinking deep from the Fountain of Peace.

Certainly, there are moments when speed must be doubled to complete a significant goal that aids others, but I will walk...*not race...*through life.

Drink deeply from the present moment; it took you a long time to get here.

7 Helpful Hints To Enjoying Your Present

1.   Cancel Any Ministry Appointment That Creates Too Much Hurry And Flurry. Space things out more. For example, I realized one morning when I awakened, that the day was going to be miserable if I rushed to get a haircut. So, I called and *rescheduled.* I breathed easier, increased the excellence of the *present* tasks I was doing, and enjoyed the day.

2.   When You Have Made An Appointment Unwisely, Give Others An Opportunity To Reschedule. Many times, I have had people to thank me for rescheduling! Their own agenda was too full. Their sense of loyalty prevented them from asking me to make a change. Changes are often better for everybody involved! "The Lord is good unto them that wait for Him, to the soul that seeketh Him. It is good that a man should both hope and quietly wait for the salvation of the Lord," (Lamentations 3:25-26).

Jesus never hurried.

3.   Do Not Rush Your Judgments Of Others. Good or bad. Someone who makes a bad first impression, may turn out to be an uncommon blessing to your life. It has been said that first impressions are lasting impressions. Of course, if that were true, divorces would never occur!

4.   Slow Down Your Eating. *Eat slowly, tasting the wonderful provision of God.* Do not hurry your eating. Doctors tell us that this is the *best* way to eat. This has been a challenge for me, personally. I am normally a very fast eater. Eating has always been an interruption, not an event. However, as The Holy Spirit has been helping me, I have been making mealtime a wonderful time of meditation, review and *thankfulness.*

5. Look For Things To Enjoy, Not Endure. What you look for, you will eventually see.

6. Look For Qualities You Love In Others, Not Qualities That Agitate You. Be thankful.

7. Concentrate On Tasks That Produce Results, Not How Many Things You Can Get Done.

Moving *decisively with purpose* is the opposite of lethargy and indifference. When you see someone move deliberately, it is not with lack of energy or caring. It is often the opposite.

Always give total attention to the task at hand. As the apostle Paul said, "Brethren, I count not myself to have apprehended: but this one thing I do, forgetting those things which are behind, and reaching forth unto those things which are before," (Philippians 3:13).

Taste Your Present; It Has Taken You A Lifetime To Get Here.

It is One of the Secrets of the Uncommon Minister.

RECOMMENDED INVESTMENTS:
Enjoying The Winning Life (Book/B-08/32 Pages/$5)
Born To Taste The Grapes (Book/B-65/32 Pages/$3)
Born To Taste The Grapes (6 Tapes/TS-13/$30)

~ 34 ~

Sit At The Feet Of The Best

―――――>―ᴏ―<――――――

Advisors Are Everywhere.

Recently, a young pastor was discussing his difficulties with me. His ministry seemed to be a collection of tragedies and disappointments.

"Who is your mentor?" I suddenly asked.

He stumbled around a bit. He seemed uneasy and uncomfortable. So, I persisted.

"Well, there is a preacher that I talk to occasionally in the next town," he answered.

"Is he truly successful?" I asked.

"No, not really, but he is someone to talk to," was his defensive reply.

I insisted that he needed a *worthy* mentor...a *capable* mentor...someone *knowledgeable.*

"Would you consider becoming my mentor?" he asked.

"I am not even a pastor! Besides I am too busy with my own Assignment of writing, speaking and traveling. You need to learn from someone who is the best at what they do—*pastoring.*"

I connected him with two friends of mine who are very successful pastors.

It is not enough to receive advice.

It is not enough to have a mentor.

You must learn the best from the Best.

When you want to improve your game of ping pong, you must play someone who is *better* than you.

When you want to increase your Wisdom, you must sit at the feet of those who *know more* than you.

Yes, this can be intimidating and uncomfortable. Yet, it is the Road to Greatness. It guarantees increase.

Many reach only for those who are accessible and *within reach.*

When I hire an attorney, I do not want someone who is merely inexpensive or near my home. I want someone who truly cares, has proven themselves in court and is known for excellence.

Some attend a church because it is near their house. How ridiculous! That is like marrying the woman who lives closer to your house than others. It is like buying a car because it is at the nearest lot.

6 Keys For Learning From The Best

1. Invest The Time Necessary To Search For Those Who Have Established An Effective Ministry. There are hair salons close to my house. Yet, I drive further to the young lady who is the best. She does it right. She is not merely accessible, she listens to me.

Pursue. Search. Find What Is *Hidden.*

2. Those Who Pursue Convenience Will Never Taste The Grapes Of Excellence. Those who are willing to inconvenience themselves in their pursuit of excellence will create the most fulfilling and uncommon life imagined.

Do not purchase clothes simply because they are "on sale." Purchase clothes that present you properly, make you feel wonderful, and cause you to want to wear them every day of your life.

3. Learning From The Best May Require A Lower Salary At The Beginning. You are in for the long-term *success,* not the short-term *salary.*

A pastor picked me up from the airport recently. He told me something interesting about his son. His son had accepted a job at a much lower salary with another pastor. The reason? That specific pastor was a superb mentor. His own success was remarkable. The young man had enough sense to accept a job with lower salary...*so that he could learn from the very best.*

4. Learning From The Best May Necessitate A Geographical Change. You might have to travel to another state. *Do it, if that is what it takes.*

5. Remember The Specific Knowledge You Are Seeking. If you are sitting at the feet of a great electrician, he may know little about protocol. However, you are not there to learn about protocol. You are there to learn about your career in electricity.

6. You Will Not Learn Everything From One Mentor During Your Life. Do not attempt to do so. This places too much stress on them as well, and you may be disappointed. God never intended for you to learn everything from one mentor. Many mentors are necessary to make you successful, learned and skilled throughout life.

Sit At The Feet Of The Best.

It is One of the Secrets of the Uncommon Minister.

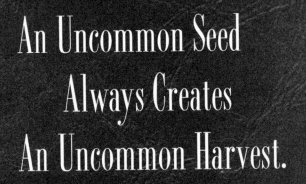

An Uncommon Seed
Always Creates
An Uncommon Harvest.

-MIKE MURDOCK

∼ 35 ∼

TEACH YOUR PEOPLE TO SOW WITH EXPECTATION OF A HARVEST

You Can Only Do What You Know.

Thousands have been taught that it is wrong to expect something in return when you give something to God. They feel that this is greed.

"When I give to God, I expect nothing in return!" is the prideful claim of many who have been taught this terrible error.

Do you *expect* a paycheck from your boss at the end of a work week? Of course, you do. Is this greed? Hardly.

Did you *expect* forgiveness when you confessed your sins to Christ? Of course, you did. Is this greed? Hardly.

Stripping expectation from your Seed is *theft* of the greatest pleasure God knows.

His greatest *pleasure* is to *believed.*

His greatest *pain* is to be *doubted.* "Without faith it is impossible to please Him: For he that cometh to God must believe that He is, and that He is a rewarder of them who diligently seek Him," (Hebrews 11:6).

Motive means *"reason* for doing something."

When someone on trial is accused of a murder, prosecutors try to find the possible motive or reason, why they were motivated to do such a horrible thing.

7 Things Every Minister Should Remember Before He Receives An Offering

1. God Uses *Harvest* As A *Motivation* For Sowing Seed.
He *expects* you to be motivated by supply, the promise of provision.

"Give, and it shall be given unto you, good measure, pressed down and shaken together, and running over, shall men give into your bosom," (Luke 6:38). This is much more than a simple principle of mercy and forgiveness. This is The Law of Harvest.

2. **God Offers *Overflow* As A *Reason* You Should Sow Seed.** "Honour the Lord with thy substance, and with the firstfruits of all thine increase: So shall thy barns be filled with plenty, and thy presses shall burst out with new wine," (Proverbs 3:9-10). Notice that He paints the picture of *overflowing* barns to *motivate* us...to give us a reason for honoring Him.

3. **God Promised *Benefits* To Those *Fearful* Of Tithing.** "Bring ye all the tithes into the storehouse, that there may be meat in Mine house, and prove Me now herewith, saith the Lord of hosts, if I will not open you the windows of heaven, and pour you out a blessing, that there shall not be room enough to receive it," (Malachi 3:10).

4. **God Paints *Portraits Of Prosperity* To Inspire Acts Of Obedience.** Read Deuteronomy 28:1-14. In these Scriptures, God creates a list of the specific blessings that will occur if you obey Him. Why does He give us these Portraits of Prosperity? To inspire and give us a reason for obedience.

Peter needed this kind of encouragement just like you and I do today. He felt such emptiness as he related to Christ that he and the others had "given up everything."

5. **Jesus Promised A *One-Hundredfold Return*.** "Then Peter began to say unto Him, Lo, we have left all, and have followed Thee. And Jesus answered and said, Verily I say unto you, There is no man that hath left house, or brethren, or sisters, or father, or mother, or wife, or children, or lands, for My sake, and the gospel's, But he shall receive an hundredfold now in this time, houses, and brethren, and sisters, and mothers, and children, and lands, with persecutions; and in the world to come eternal life," (Mark 10:28-30).

Many people think it is evil to sow Seed for a desired Harvest. Ridiculous! *Harvest is the reason for sowing!* Giving is the cure for greed. When you sow, you have just mastered greed. Greed *hoards*. Man *withholds*. Satan *steals*.

6. **The Nature Of God Alone Is *Giving*.** When you give, you have just revealed the nature of God is within you.

7. The Only Pleasure God Receives Is Through Acts Of Faith. I stress this again. His *only* need is to be believed. His *greatest* need is to be believed. "God is not a man that He should lie; neither the son of man, that He should repent: hath He said, and shall He not do it? or hath He spoken, and shall He not make it good?" (Numbers 23:19).

Suppose an unbeliever approaches you after church and says, "I want to give my heart to Christ, Pastor." Suppose the unbeliever then says, "Will you pray that God will give me peace and forgiveness for my confession?"

Imagine yourself replying with indignation, "Of course not! That is greedy. You want something in return for giving your heart to Christ?" They would be shocked by such a reaction.

Your Heavenly Father offers Supply for Seed; Forgiveness for Confession; Order for Chaos.

When Jesus talked to the woman at the well of Samaria, He promised her water that she would never thirst again. Was He wrong to offer her something if she pursued Him? Of course not. That was the purpose of the portrait of water—to motivate her and *give her a reason for obeying Him.*

One day, a dear friend, who is a powerful evangelist, told me a story about the papaya. Somebody counted 470 papaya seeds in a single papaya. If that was consistent, one papaya seed will produce a plant containing ten papayas. If each of the ten contained 470 seeds, there would be 4,700 papaya seeds on one plant.

Now, just suppose you replant those 4,700 seeds to create 4,700 more plants. Do you know how much 5,000 plants containing 5,000 seeds would be? *Twenty-five million seeds...on the second planting alone.* Yet, we are having difficulty over really believing in the hundredfold return. Why?

Millions must *unlearn* the poisonous and traitorous teaching that it is wrong to expect anything in return.

A businessman approached me. "I do not really believe Jesus really meant what He said about the hundredfold. We have misunderstood that." "So, you intend to teach Jesus how to talk when you get to heaven?" I laughed.

If God will do it for a papaya...He will do it for you and me. We are His children, not merely fruit on a tree!

I believe one of the major reasons people do not experience a supernatural, abundant Harvest of Finances is because they really do not expect Jesus to do what He said He would do.

8 Facts You Should Teach Your People About Expectation

1.   Expectation Is The Current That Makes The Seed Work For You. "But without faith it is impossible to please Him: for he that cometh to God must believe that He is, and that He is a rewarder of them that diligently seek Him," (Hebrews 11:6).

2.   Expect Protection As God Promised. "And I will rebuke the devourer for your sakes, and he shall not destroy the fruits of your ground; neither shall your vine cast her fruit before the time in the field, saith the Lord of hosts," (Malachi 3:11).

3.   Expect Favor From A Boaz Close To You. "Give, and it shall be given unto you; good measure, pressed down, and shaken together, and running over, shall men give into your bosom. For with the same measure that ye mete withal it shall be measured to you again," (Luke 6:38).

4.   Expect Financial Ideas And Wisdom. "But thou shalt remember the Lord thy God: for it is He that giveth thee power to get wealth," (Deuteronomy 8:18).

5.   Expect Your Enemies To Be Confused And Flee Before You. "The Lord shall cause thine enemies that rise up against thee to be smitten before thy face: they shall come out against thee one way, and flee before thee seven ways," (Deuteronomy 28:7).

6.   Expect God To Bless You For Every Act Of Obedience. "And it shall come to pass, if thou shalt hearken diligently unto the voice of the Lord thy God, to observe and to do all His commandments which I command thee this day, that the Lord thy God will set thee on high above all nations of the earth: And all these blessings shall come on thee, and overtake thee, if thou shalt hearken unto the voice of the Lord thy God," (Deuteronomy 28:1-2).

7.   Expectation Affects God. When you sow with expectation, your Seed will stand before God as a testimony of your faith and confidence.

> ▶   Sow, expecting God to respond favorably to every act of confidence in Him.

▶ Sow, from *every* paycheck.

▶ Sow, expectantly, generously and faithfully.

8. When You Start Looking And Expecting God To Fulfill His Promise, The Harvest You Have Needed So Long Will Come More Quickly And Bountifully Than You Have Ever Dreamed.

Our Prayer Together...

"Father, teach me the Wonder of Expectation. Show me how it pleasures You to be believed. Hasten the Harvest as I depend on Your incredible integrity. Show me how to unlock the expectations of my people so they can taste the rewards of an Uncommon Harvest. In Jesus' name. Amen."

Teach Your People To Sow With Expectation Of A Harvest.

It is One of the Secrets of the Uncommon Minister.

RECOMMENDED INVESTMENTS:

Seeds of Wisdom on Seed-Faith, Volume 4 (Book/B-16/32 Pages/$3)

31 Reasons People Do Not Receive Their Financial Harvest (Book/B-82/ 252 Pages/$12)

31 Reasons People Do Not Receive Their Financial Harvest (6 Tapes/TS-38/$30)

You Cannot Have A Great Life
Unless You Have A Pure Life;
You Cannot Have A Pure Life
Unless You Have A Pure Mind;
You Cannot Have A Pure Mind
Unless You Wash It Daily
With The Word Of God.

-MIKE MURDOCK

⌘ 36 ⌘

ESTABLISH YOUR SECRET PLACE FOR MEETING PRIVATELY WITH THE HOLY SPIRIT EACH DAY

The Secret Place Will Birth Change In You.

An Uncommon Experience Births An *Uncommon Ministry.* The Secret Place is the place where you meet with God every day of your life.

It is where you enter His presence and are loved, corrected, informed and changed. It is the Room where you kneel in humility at the Altar of Mercy and receive forgiveness, restoration and revelation regarding your Assignment on earth.

It is your Prayer Room. It is the prayer closet, or any place you have sanctified and set apart for the *exclusive use of The Holy Spirit* to deal privately and intimately with your life.

Establishing your *Secret Place* is possibly the most life changing, revolutionizing decision you will make during your lifetime, if you correctly discern the dramatic encounters such a place can birth.

15 Keys To Entering The Secret Place

1. **Enter Daily.** The Psalmist said, "Lord, I have called daily upon Thee, I have stretched out my hands unto Thee," (Psalm 88:9).

2. **Enter Your Secret Place When Your Ministry Is Threatened Or Abused.** "The angel of the Lord encampeth round about them that fear Him, and delivereth them," (Psalm 34:7).

3. **Enter Before Making Any Major Financial Decisions About Your Ministry.** The apostle Paul understood this. "But my God shall supply all your need according to His riches in glory by Christ Jesus," (Philippians 4:19).

4. **Enter Confessing Your Personal Weaknesses And**

Expect To Be Made Strong. Jesus is still the difference in your ministry. "I can do all things through Christ which strengtheneth me," (Philippians 4:13).

5. **Enter With A Broken And Contrite Spirit.** Humility is the magnet that never fails to attract God. "The Lord is nigh unto them that are of a broken heart; and saveth such as be of a contrite spirit," (Psalm 34:18).

6. **Enter When You Feel Disappointed Concerning Unanswered Prayers.** It worked for the greatest king of Israel. "Therefore David said unto his servants, Is the child dead? And they said, He is dead. Then David arose from the earth, and washed, and anointed himself, and changed his apparel, and came into the house of the Lord, and worshiped," (2 Samuel 12:19-20).

7. **Enter When You Need Acts Of Mercy From God.** It was the secret of David's anointing. "Great deliverance giveth He to His king; and sheweth mercy to His anointed, to David, and to his seed for evermore," (Psalm 18:50).

8. **Enter If You Have Fallen Deep Into Personal Sin.** Reaching is the remedy for a preacher's sins, too! "The steps of a good man are ordered by the Lord: and he delighteth in His way. Though he fall, he shall not be utterly cast down: for the Lord upholdeth him with His hand," (Psalm 37:23-24).

9. **Enter When Someone Is Speaking Slanderous Words Which Are Stirring Up Enmity And Strife Against You.** The arms of God are always your best defense. "Thou shalt hide them in the secret of Thy presence from the pride of man: Thou shalt keep them secretly in a pavilion from the strife of tongues," (Psalm 31:20).

10. **Enter When Your Ministry Is Encountering Confusion And Unexpected Change.** Transition is often our most vulnerable season. "My times are in Thy hand: deliver me from the hand of mine enemies, and from them that persecute me," (Psalm 31:15).

11. **Enter When You Are Uncertain In Your Decision-Making.** Consulting God is never a mistake. "I will instruct thee and teach thee in the way which thou shalt go: I will guide thee with Mine eye," (Psalm 32:8).

12. **Enter When Money Problems Are Strangling Your Ministry.** God wants your ministry to prosper. "Now ye Philippians know also, that in the beginning of the gospel, when I departed from

Macedonia, no church communicated with me as concerning giving and receiving, but ye only. But I have all, and abound: I am full, having received of Epaphroditus the things which were sent from you, an odour of a sweet smell, a sacrifice acceptable, wellpleasing to God," (Philippians 4:15, 18).

13. Enter Into His Presence When Your Ministry Is Doing Well. The goodness of God deserves recognition. "I will bless the Lord at all times: His praise shall continually be in my mouth. My soul shall make her boast in the Lord: the humble shall hear thereof, and be glad," (Psalm 34:1-2).

14. Enter Into His Presence When Your Dreams And Goals Seem Impossible To Achieve. God loves to do the impossible. "O fear the Lord, ye His saints: for there is no want to them that fear Him. The young lions do lack, and suffer hunger: but they that seek the Lord shall not want any good thing," (Psalm 34:9-10).

15. Enter With Expectation. God honors it. "For he that cometh to God must believe that He is, and that He is a rewarder of them that diligently seek Him," (Hebrews 11:6).

Expectation is a current. It sweeps you into the Holy Place. It brings you into God's presence where you are purged, purified and changed.

Expect God to *respond* to you.

Expect pain to *leave* your body.

Expect *confusion* to depart from your mind.

Expect *revelation* concerning those you love.

Expect supernatural *peace* and *joy* to explode within your heart as you enter His presence.

Establish Your Secret Place For Meeting Privately With The Holy Spirit Each Day.

It is One of the Secrets of the Uncommon Minister.

RECOMMENDED INVESTMENTS:
The Mentor's Manna on The Secret Place (Book/B-78/32 Pages/$3)
The Holy Spirit Handbook Volume 1 (Book/B-100/153 Pages/$15)
Love Songs to The Holy Spirit, Series 1 (6 Tapes/TS-59/$30)

Your Understanding Of God Determines Your Message To Men.

-MIKE MURDOCK

⮞ 37 ⮜

PREACH TO REVEAL THE GREATNESS OF GOD

God Is The Only Answer To Life.

You know it. Others do not. Their focus is on their problem. Your focus is on their solution.

Connect People To God. The apostle Paul understood this. "Whereof I was made a minister...that I should preach among the Gentiles the unsearchable riches of Christ; And to make all men see what is the fellowship of the mystery, which from the beginning of the world hath been hid in God, who created all things by Jesus Christ: To the intent that now unto the principalities and powers in heavenly places might be known by the church the manifold Wisdom of God, According to the eternal purpose which he purposed in Christ Jesus our Lord," (Ephesians 3:7-11).

4 Facts About Preaching

1. **Preaching Is A Simple Political Weapon, Position Or Belief.**
2. **Preaching Is Not A Forum For Your Prejudices.**
3. **Preaching Is The Oil, That Heals The Wounded.**
4. **Preaching Is The Bridge Out Of Trouble.**

How To Know If Your Preaching Is A Success Or Failure

When your people leave a service discussing the greatness of God, you have *succeeded.*

When they leave discussing your preaching skills, you have *failed.*

When your people leave excited and enthused over their future, you have *succeeded.*

When they walk out of the service fearful and perplexed, you have *failed.*

10 Miracles That Preaching Produces

1. **Preach God So *Big* Your People Can No Longer See You In The Pulpit.**

2. **Preach God So *Powerful* The Mountains Your People Face Appear As Pebbles Compared To The Greatness Of Their God.**

3. **Preach God So *Good* Your People Want Their Friends To Experience His Goodness.**

4. **Preach God So *Merciful* Your People Expect The Most Sinful Around Them To Be Changed.**

5. **Preach God So *Loving* Your People Do Not Want To Leave His Presence.**

6. **Preach God So *Forgiving* Your People Refuse To Hide Their Sins.**

7. **Preach God So *Just* The Anger Of Your People Subsides.**

8. **Preach God So *Healing* That Sickness And Disease Cannot Survive Among Your People.**

9. **Preach God So *Providing* That The Financial Chains Of Your People Are Broken.**

10. **Preach God So *Accessible* That Your People Build A Secret Place In Their Home To Meet With Him Daily.**

Preach To Reveal The Greatness Of God.

It is One of the Secrets of the Uncommon Minister.

≈ 38 ≈

KNOW YOUR STAFF WELL

Your Future Is Affected By Your Staff.
A *careless* staff will destroy your *dream.*
An *uncaring* staff will destroy your *motivation.*
An *untaught* staff will paralyze your *progress.*
An *arrogant* staff will alienate your friends.
"...know them which labour among you," (1 Thessalonians 5:12).
Jesus knew His disciples well. He spoke to Peter, "Satan hath desired to have you, that he may sift you as wheat: But I have prayed for thee, that thy faith fail not: and when thou art converted, strengthen thy brethren," (Luke 22:31-32).

6 Things To Know About Your Staff

1. Know The Dominant Gifts And Skills Of Your Staff. Who is the most qualified to motivate others? Repair a computer? Show hospitality to visitors? Type your letter? Find flaws in your manuscripts? Who can get things done the easiest? Who has leadership skills? Whose loyalty keeps everything bonded together around you? Their gifts and skills were planted there by The Holy Spirit for the completion of your work and calling. (Read Exodus 31:1-6.)

2. Know The Background Of Your Staff. A pastor friend of mine was troubled. "Mike, my Minister of Music simply will not learn new songs that I want him to learn. I have pushed, encouraged and even gotten a little angry. Yet, he simply will not change." As we talked, it dawned on him that the *background* of this Minister of Music was much different than his. He had no feeling for the new songs of praise and worship. He was comfortable with traditional songs. You see, our background has everything to do with our comfort, prejudices and fears. Knowing your staff is vitally important.

3.   Know The Greatest Fears Of Your Staff. After much discussion, I discovered that one of my associate's greatest fears was the loss of consistent income. His bitter experiences of the past made him very fearful of any job loss. Just the thought of being fired almost paralyzed him with fear. He did not have the confidence that he could find another job easily.

In an interview, a new candidate for a position on my staff expressed concern. According to our policy handbook, they were required to wait ninety days before securing medical insurance. That was troubling. Why? They greatly feared a sudden tragedy, disease or sickness would catch them "unprotected."

Your fears affect your decision-making. That is why it is essential that you know the greatest fears of the leaders of your staff. I had a manager who feared firing an employee. Years before, he had experienced a lawsuit because of the firing of an obnoxious employee. It left him devastated and overly cautious. Consequently, he retained one of my employees much too long because he feared another legal battle.

4.   Know The Weaknesses Of Your Staff. I had a tragic experience. One of my favorite friends had supposedly mastered a drug problem. So, I finally accepted him as a travel assistant to help strengthen and build him up again in the work of the Lord. He assured me that he had not touched drugs in several years. I believed him. Late one night, he and I arrived at a southern city. The pastor and several of his board members met us at the airport and took us back to the hotel. Just past midnight, after we finished praying together in my room, he returned to his own suite. The next morning, I could not locate him. He was not in his room. I rode in the car to the church with a perplexed and heavy heart. Something was wrong. I knew it.

That morning, several members of my staff had driven over two hundred miles to the service. They were puzzled by his disappearance, also. That afternoon, he never appeared. That night, as I finished the crusade, he was still absent. When the pastor and his men took me to the airport Monday morning, I apologized and said, "I think I know what is wrong, but, I am not free to discuss it now." I was embarrassed beyond description.

Three days later, my travel associate telephoned. He was cheerful and lighthearted about his "mistake." He had found some friends, taken drugs and was "out" on them for three days. Obviously,

I could not take him back into my home and my ministry. He was upset by this fact. However, his sin had become a very small and playful thing to him.

The pastor and church? He is still one of my favorite pastors. I love the church. Even so, the embarrassment to my ministry has been so great I have been too uncomfortable to return to the church.

Some Weaknesses Of Your Staff Are Capable Of Destroying *Every* Dream God Has Placed In Your Heart. That is why Achan was stoned. That is why The Holy Spirit killed Ananias in the church. That is why Korah was swallowed up in the earth.

Your ministry cannot succeed beyond the weaknesses of your staff. Know them. Name them. Correct them. Help your staff overcome them. Do not stay ignorant of their weaknesses.

Know those who *exaggerate.*

Know those who *lie.*

Know those who speak *disloyalty* behind your back.

Know those who are *envious* of your success as the leader.

Know those who will pour out their life for you.

Know those who truly work *for* you. "...know them which labour among you," (1 Thessalonians 5:12). Reward The Loyal.

5.   **Know The Friends Of Your Staff.** Someone else is speaking into the lives of your staff, also. You are not their *only* advisor.

Yesterday, a young pastor sat here in my home. He was troubled. He had lost two of his favorite people from his staff. As we talked, it became evident that two other friends had caused their agitation. Their *offenses* were *fueled.* As soon as a door opened, they scattered.

Friends are photographs of our *comfort zone.* Your staff may love you. They may like you. However, their friends are possibly telling them *much more* than you are speaking into their lives. What are the weaknesses of those friends? Think for a moment. What is the passion level of the friends of your staff? What does your staff do for *recreation?* With whom do they shop? These are clues to their life.

6.   **Know The Heroes Of Your Staff.** Everybody follows somebody. Whose books do they read? Whose achievements do they admire?

Know Your Staff Well.

It is One of the Secrets of the Uncommon Minister.

Information That Is Not Retrievable Is Unusable.

-MIKE MURDOCK

❧ 39 ❧

KEEP A RECEIPT FOR EVERY MINISTRY PURCHASE

Document Every Purchase.

Sometimes, it may not seem to be important. Yet, it is very important that you develop the habit of keeping receipts on everything that you buy. When I leave the airport, I secure a receipt for the fifty-cent cost, not because I am desperate for the reimbursement. I need the *habit* of asking for a receipt to be emphasized and made permanent in my life. I want the habit to become *instinctive,* not requiring my memory or attention.

Something interesting happened many years ago. When I left a hotel in Kentucky, I pulled out my credit card to pay for my telephone calls. Usually, the church pays for the room and food. I always pay for the telephone calls, faxes or other items. I was in a hurry to leave for the airport. I placed the receipt in my little leather bag.

In those days, I would often preach several weeks of meetings before returning home. Receipts pile up. After a few weeks, you collect a stack of receipts that you cannot begin to explain to anyone! Especially when you are taking flights, shoving $5.00 bills in the hands of a bellman at the hotel...the hands of a skycap at the airport. When you are busy making change and running through airports, receipts become a blur. (Since then, I try to *write something on every receipt* that explains it so that it will trigger my memory two or three weeks later while reviewing it with my bookkeeper.)

Thirty days later, the telephone rang. I was in my little garage working at my desk. It was my office at the time in Houston, Texas. My pastor friend from Kentucky was on the phone. He sounded rather distant and cool.

"Hello, Mike? I just wanted to know why you did not pay your own telephone calls here at the hotel when you checked out?" He did not even bother *asking* me if I had paid the hotel for the telephone bill or not. He plunged in with full confidence that the hotel personnel had given him accurate information.

I was taken back. In fact, I felt rather agitated that he had not questioned me first. The telephone bill was not that high. I explained to him that I *had* paid my own telephone bill.

"Well, they have just charged the church for it again, if you did pay it."

I asked him to hold the line for a few moments. I began to dig through my desk drawer for the credit card receipt. Miraculously, it was still in the stack of receipts. I pulled it out and gave the details to him on the phone. Then, I made a copy and mailed it to him. (This was before the days of fax machines! How I bless the person who created the fax machine!)

My receipt salvaged my reputation. However, he was so embarrassed over his attitude toward me that he never again had the courage and comfort to approach me about a crusade. I had been speaking for him every year. The meetings were tremendous.

The receipt episode damaged our relationship.

The Retrieval System Protected My Reputation.

5 Benefits Of Keeping Receipts

1. **The Habit Of Keeping Receipts Will Help You With Your Taxes.** When you complete your income tax forms at the end of the year, you will be thankful for every receipt that can save you money.

2. **Keeping Receipts Keeps You Reminded Of Where Your Money Has Been Spent.** This is important. Expenses are always much more than what you had planned. Keeping receipts helps you in budgeting and thinking ahead.

3. **Keeping Receipts Can Protect Your Reputation Of Integrity.** When you keep receipts, you can prove your honesty.

4. **When You Keep Receipts, You Send A Message Of Organization And Order.** You know what you are talking about, and it shows.

5. **When You Keep Receipts, You Increase The Confidence Of Others Toward You.** They will consider your opinion valuable on other matters as well.

When an employee approaches my bookkeeper for a reimbursement *without* a receipt, this sends a message to me.

Were they sloppy in their organizing of receipts?

Did they really secure a receipt?

Did they actually spend the money?

Are they unconcerned about the finances of the ministry?

The answer? Simple. Get a receipt.

6 Things Are Revealed When You Fail To Secure Receipts

1. **You Portray Sloppiness And Disorder.**
2. **You Send A Message Of Rebellion, Instead Of Excellence.**
3. **You Cause Others To Doubt Your Words.**
4. **You Slow Down Reimbursements.**
5. **You Invite Scrutiny And Investigation.**
6. **You Create A Climate Of Suspicion.**

Solomon was meticulous about record keeping. Every single animal was accounted for that was used in a meal in the palace. "Be thou diligent to know the state of thy flocks, and look well to thy herds," (Proverbs 27:23). Why? "For riches are not for ever," (Proverbs 27:24).

Keep A Receipt For Every Ministry Purchase.

It is One of the Secrets of the Uncommon Minister.

The Only Reason
Men Fail Is
Broken Focus.

-MIKE MURDOCK

❧ 40 ❧

GIVE YOUR TOTAL ATTENTION TO THE IMMEDIATE MOMENT

Focus Produces Miracles.

Whatever receives your focus will grow, improve and multiply. Whatever you give attention to will *increase* and become better.

Many years ago, I was helped by the marvelous insight of one of my dearest friends, Donna Douglas, a well-known celebrity. Millions still know her as Ellie Mae Clampett on "The Beverly Hillbillies." Her scrapbooks were thick and piled high regarding her fame. Thousands of photographers had photographed her. Yet, I noticed that when people talked to her, she looked straight into their eyes. She gave them her complete attention. Her schedule was full, but she always *abandoned herself to the moment* when conversing with others.

She explained it simply. *"Mike, I am always wherever I am."* She refused to let her mind be in a different place than her body.

Here is how it helped her:

When she conversed with someone, she gave total focus to every word they said. Consequently, her *reactions* were accurate for that moment. Her perception was pure. Her instincts were *incredible*. The person always received *the best* of what she possessed at that moment. Afterwards, it was unnecessary for her to replay the conversation to see if she had forgotten to say the right things, *remember* the right information or have *any* regrets. They had received the best that she had. The moment ended. It was over. *Now, her future received her undivided attention.*

She was always where she was.

This helped me greatly. You see, many are thinking about their home and family while they are at work. So, their best work *never* emerges. They never taste the results of *total* focus. They never reach maximum quality in anything they do on their job. They are not *really* where they are. Their mind is elsewhere.

So, when they finally arrive home, their family *still* does not receive their total focus. They mentally replay their day at their job, hoping they did not forget anything. Subconsciously, it is a burden which produces stress. Their mind is always in a different place than their body and efforts.

4 Keys To Complete Focus On The Immediate Moment

1.   Always Be Wherever You Are.
Have you ever attended a conference and enjoyed fellowship with others? Have you ever talked to someone who was busy *looking around the room* while you were trying to tell them something that happened? It unsettled you. Their eyes were upon *others,* while you were trying to keep their attention. Yet, moments before, they were talking to *someone else* looking for you! Now, they are talking to you...looking for someone else!

This is what happens every day of our lives.

When I teach, I refuse to think about my office and staff. My focus is that service and the people before me. *This frees me.* When I was a young preacher, I would replay the concluded service in my mind over and over again. Today is different. I now realize that I have poured my best into that service. When I leave, the service is over. Now, I am released to give total attention *to my future.*

2.   Always Give Your Highest Wisdom To The Immediate Conversation. Listen carefully. Reply with caution. Insist on accuracy, tact and kindness.

3.   Always Give The Highest Quality Of Thought To Every Conversation. Think thoroughly before you respond to questions, problems or controversy.

4.   Develop Habitual Excellence In Every Moment. Potential problems will then not worry you. You have developed excellence *with each moment.* Tomorrow can become another performance of excellence, *which you have been practicing* every moment of today. This explains why Jesus said, "And when they bring you unto the synagogues, and unto magistrates, and powers, take ye no thought how or what thing ye shall answer, or what ye shall say: For the Holy Ghost shall teach you in the same hour what ye ought to say," (Luke 12:11-12).

Give Your Total Attention To The Immediate Moment.

It is One of the Secrets of the Uncommon Minister.

～ 41 ～

IDENTIFY YOUR PERSONAL GREATNESS

You Contain An Uncommon Treasure.

It is invisible but irrefutable. It is your difference, your dominant gifting and the magnet drawing others.

It is your *greatness*. "But we have this treasure in earthen vessels, that the excellency of the power may be of God, and not of us," (2 Corinthians 4:7).

God knows it. He created you. He has always known the invisible purpose for which you were created.

Something about your ministry is irreplaceable.

What is it?

8 Things You Should Know About Your Greatness

1.   Your Assignment To Preach Was Decided In Your Mother's Womb. "Before I formed thee in the belly I knew thee; and before thou camest forth out of the womb I sanctified thee, and I ordained thee a prophet unto the nations," (Jeremiah 1:5).

You are not an accident waiting to happen.

"I will praise Thee; for I am fearfully and wonderfully made: marvellous are Thy works; and that my soul knoweth right well," (Psalm 139:14).

2.   Everything Inside You Is Known, Treasured And Intended For Full Use By Your Creator. "My substance was not hid from Thee, when I was made in secret, and curiously wrought in the lowest parts of the earth," (Psalm 139:15).

3.   Your Flaws Do Not Necessarily Prevent God From Using You In Ministry. They exist to motivate your pursuit of Him.

"Thine eyes did see my substance, yet being unperfect; and in Thy book all my members were written, which in continuance were fashioned, when as yet there was none of them," (Psalm 139:16).

4. Your Very Existence Was Strategized By God. "How precious also are Thy thoughts unto me, O God! how great is the sum of them! If I should count them, they are more in number than the sand: when I awake, I am still with Thee," (Psalm 139:17-18).

Picture an author exulting over his book. The book exists. The author created it. He is excited about it whether anyone else is or not. Imagine a composer, exhilarated over a completed song. He knew its beginning and its ending. Its potential excites him.

5. Your Very Presence Energizes God. He saw your beginning and His desired conclusion.

God is looking at something within you that *you have never seen.*

- ▶ God is looking at something inside you that even *satan cannot discern.*
- ▶ God is looking at something you contain that *you have not yet discovered.*
- ▶ God will tell you secrets satan will never hear.
- ▶ The mercies of God have not been wasted on you and your ministry. He has big plans for your life.

The forgiveness of God has validated your ministry. You are *becoming* a monument and trophy of His grace. God boasts about you and your ministry to every demon who enters His presence. (Read Job 1:8.)

- ▶ You are looking at your *beginning.*
  God is looking at your *end.*
- ▶ You are studying your *flaws.*
  God is studying your *future.*
- ▶ You are studying your *enemies.*
  God is studying your *eventuality.*
- ▶ You are awaiting your *destiny.*
  God is awaiting your *discovery of it.*

6. Never Consult Those Who Have Not Discovered The Greatness Within You. Their focus will be different, their conclusions inaccurate, their counsel useless.

7. Stay In The Presence Of The One Who Created You.

You will never quit feeling good about yourself when you stay in His presence. He is looking at something He considers to be remarkable. He planted this greatness within you while you were yet in your mother's womb.

David discerned his greatness and willingly confronted Goliath.

Soldiers saw brashness; The Holy Spirit saw *boldness*.

Soldiers saw anger; God saw justice.

Joseph discerned his greatness.

His brothers saw pride; God saw *passion*.

The brothers saw a threat; God saw a *throne*.

8. The Opinion And Observation Of Others Is Not The Foundation For Your Greatness. So, stop pursuing their approval. God is looking at something inside you they *cannot* see, *refuse* to see and may *never* see.

The brothers of Jesus could not discern His *Divinity*.

The brothers of Joseph could not *interpret his dream* properly.

The brothers of David could not *imagine him* as a soldier.

The friends of Job could not discern the satanic scenario *before his crisis*.

Haman could not even discern the nationality of Esther.

Nobody is completely accurate in their assessment of you. *Nobody*.

Your flaws are *much less* than they imagine.

Your greatness is *far greater* than they will ever discern.

The Holy Spirit *alone* has accurately assessed your *future*, your *passion*, and the *willingness* of your heart to become great. That is why He keeps reaching, pursuing and developing you in the midst of every attack and crisis.

God never *gives up* on you.

God never *quits looking* at you.

God never *changes His plans* toward you.

God never quits believing in your future.

Remember this continuously, God is seeing something inside you that keeps Him excited and involved. It is something nobody else can see.

Find Your Greatness.

It is One of the Secrets of the Uncommon Minister.

Those Who Ask
The Questions
Determine The Quality
Of The Conversation.

-MIKE MURDOCK

☞ 42 ☜

TEACH YOUR PEOPLE THE POWER OF ASKING

Asking Is The Key To Receiving.

Jesus made this very clear. "Ask, and it shall be given you; seek, and you shall find; knock, and it shall be opened unto you. For everyone that asketh receiveth; and he that seeketh findeth; and to him that knocketh it shall be opened," (Matthew 7:7-8).

Many *desire* more money.

Many *wish* for more money.

Many *dream* about more money.

Yet, they never have understood the *power of asking,* and asking *specifically.*

"I really need more money," one elderly lady told me late one night after a lecture.

"How much are you needing?" I asked.

"Oh, I just need more!"

She was even more persistent. "I just need more, that is all!"

Finally, I pulled a nickel out of my pocket and handed it to her saying, "Your prayers just got answered." You see, she wanted more, and I gave her more. However, she never asked for a *specific* amount.

9 Reasons People Do Not Receive What They Desire

1.   **Many Rebel Against Asking.** Asking is an agitation to them. You see, asking really is a portrait of humility. When you ask somebody for something, you are admitting lack and limitation. That is not taught in our society today.

Self-confidence is often the currency in the world of success.

Asking is considered to be a weakness. Yet, it is the Golden Key to receiving.

2.   Many Refuse To Ask God For A Financial Harvest.
Why? They have disobeyed Him and every instruction He has given and know it. This destroys their bravado and boldness. You can only be bold when you know you are right.

When you have ignored faithful church attendance, tithing and putting God first, you usually lack the audacity to approach Him for anything. It is very difficult to spend Sundays on your boat in the lake and then feel comfortable to ask Him for money on Monday morning.

3.   Many Refuse To Ask God For Specific Amounts Of Income. Why? They do not know how much they even owe their creditors.

Many years ago a young man came to me in desperation. He said, "I am going bankrupt. I am going to lose everything I have. Would you help me?"

"Tell me exactly how much you owe your creditors," I replied.

He looked puzzled and bewildered. "I have no idea how much money I owe."

"Well, sit down and make me a list of each person that you owe, the amount you owe them, and how much you can set aside each month to pay them off completely."

He took the conversation another direction. I brought him back to it.

"Stop beating around the bush. Sit down and make me a list of what you actually owe. You cannot use your faith without a target. *Faith requires an instruction.* If faith has an option, it will not work. Faith must be given a specific Assignment." "A double minded man is unstable in all his ways," (James 1:8).

4.   Many Refuse To Ask God In Faith. They whine, cry and even weep bitterly in church services. Yet, they refuse to wrap their request with the garments of faith and *expectation.* "Without faith it is impossible to please Him: for he that cometh to God must believe that He is, and that He is a rewarder of them that diligently seek Him," (Hebrews 11:6).

God wants to be believed. God's Only Pain Is To Be Doubted; God's Only Pleasure Is To Be Believed. Every effort of God has one focus—to find a person who believes what He says.

▶   God has an obsession *to be believed.*

▶   God *destroys* those who doubt.

▶ God *rewards* those who believe. (Read Deuteronomy 28:1-14.)

Tears alone do not move God.

Desperation does not move God.

Manipulation does not move God.

Education does not influence God.

Faith is the only force that impresses God to do miracles. You must ask in faith. Faith comes when you hear God talk. "So then faith cometh by hearing, and hearing by the word of God," (Romans 10:17).

5. Some Do Not Ask Because They Believe That Provision Is Sovereign, Based On The Whim Or Impulses Of God.

"Mike, if God wants me to have money, He will give it to me."

So, I replied to this brother, "That means, had He wanted you to comb your hair this morning, He would have combed it for you. If He wanted you to wear clothes, you would not have been born naked." How absurd! God wants everyone saved, doesn't He? Yet, many are going to hell. Your will is involved. *Provision is a choice.*

6. Some Do Not Ask God For A Financial Harvest Because They Believe That Money Is A Trap.

"Don't you think satan gives people a lot of money, so they will go back on God?"

I replied to this lady, "If money can make you backslide, why hasn't satan overdosed you with it?" If money could cause you to move away from God, satan would back a semi-truck to your house and unload $100 bills all over your yard.

7. Many Never Ask God For Financial Wisdom. They never enter The Secret Place before making major purchases such as a house or an automobile. They never consider fasting three days before accepting a new job. They depend on their own mind and perception. They ignore The Holy Spirit who will advise them in all things.

The early disciples asked The Holy Spirit about *everything,* even the places they should minister. Read these fascinating words, "As they ministered to the Lord, and fasted, the Holy Ghost said, Separate me Barnabus and Paul for the work whereunto I have called them. And when they had fasted and prayed, and laid their hands on them, they sent them away. So they, being sent forth by the Holy

Ghost, departed unto Seleucia; and from thence they sailed to Cyprus," (Acts 13:2-4).

They were not moved by the needs of people.

They were moved by *the Voice of The Spirit*.

They did not go where they were needed.

They went where they were *commanded*.

8.   Many Refuse To Ask For A Specific Miracle.

"I really need a house," said a young man one night.

"Describe the house you are asking God to provide," was my reply.

"Oh, just anything; I just need a house."

You know, God could have given him a dog house and he would not be able to complain.

If you are asking God for a specific house, peruse magazines until you find exactly the house you have been asking God to provide. *Focus your faith for it.*

If you are asking God for a specific automobile, find the color, the model and the specific car in some magazine and hold that page up to God in intercession daily and claim it in your future.

If you are asking God for a specific financial miracle, post the amount on your bulletin board. Inform your circle of intercessors. Hold that sheet of paper high in prayer during your seasons of intercession.

Clarify. Be specific. Focus your faith with precision. Faith will not respond to an *uncertain sound*. God responds to directness. Persistence. Tenacity.

9.   Few Really Know What They Want Financially Out Of Life. Precision is rare in conversations. I have sat at restaurant tables while friends have looked into the face of a waitress they have never met in their life and asked, "What do you think I should eat today?" It puzzles me.

I have seen friends purchase clothes that the *salesman* liked! In fact, it was a salesman that they had never even met before in their lifetime. Think about it! Someone they had never met, making decisions about the clothes they are wearing!

When you ask God for anything:

Ask *specifically.*

Ask *persistently.*

Ask *expectantly.*

Ask *largely.*
Ask *honestly.*
Teach Your People The Power Of Asking.
It is One of the Secrets of the Uncommon Minister.

RECOMMENDED INVESTMENT:
31 Reasons People Do Not Receive Their Financial Harvest (Book/B-82/
 252 Pages/$12)

The Presence Of God Is
The Only Place Where
Your Weakness Will Die.

-MIKE MURDOCK

～ 43 ～

BECOME A WORSHIPER YOURSELF

Praise Creates Internal Enthusiasm.

It is 8:35 a.m. this Thursday morning...went to bed about 3:00 a.m. this morning. I was awakened about 20 minutes ago to a pounding in my spirit of the song, "I will bless the Lord at all times...His praise shall continually be in my mouth."

You must partake of the manna you tell others about.

Worship is one of the Secrets of Fulfilling ministry.

Preachers can become calloused and insensitive to God because of concentrating on others. I have observed, with sadness that some ministers even prefer to converse in their offices rather than enter worship time with their people.

5 Keys For Becoming A Worshiper

1. **You Must *Personally* Bless The Lord.** Nobody else can do it for you. You must praise Him. Your *people* cannot do it for you.

2. ***You* Must Bless The Lord.** You must purpose in your heart. Make a decision. *Determine* to do it. Become tenacious and persistent about it. Set your mind in agreement with it.

3. **You Must *Bless* The Lord.** He has blessed you! Everything around you shows blessing. His health and healing flows through your being. Your mind throbs with motivation. Your heart is full of dreams and goals. He is worthy of your blessing Him...honoring Him...bringing Him glory.

4. **You Must Bless *The Lord Himself*.** Many request attention. Others pull at your strength, your attention, your life, your time and your energy.

Letters are thrust in my father's face..."Make sure Dr. Murdock gets this personally." Telephone calls come to my friends in the middle of the night. "Tell Dr. Mike this for me."

Yet, I refuse to permit anybody around me *to become The Priority Focus of my life*. I was created for Him...*for Him*. When He dominates my life, only then do I have something worthwhile to give to others, minister to them and feed them. If I permit others to become mere parasites in my life, they will not be sustained. *Both* of us will be destroyed.

If God is my focus, everything else I do will *multiply and prosper. Others* will increase *because of it*.

You must bless *the Lord*. He is the precious Holy Spirit Who walks beside you. Your Advisor and Counselor. Your Best Friend. The One Who knows all things. He *remembers* every word that Jesus spoke, and He reminds you so that you can "enter into the life of Christ."

Spirit Focus is not always easy. Others may *always attempt* to be the focus. They need attention. They require fueling and energy from you.

Others will interpret *withdrawal as rejection*. But, if God is not your focus, your mind *loses* its peace. Your heart *loses* its joy. Your ministry *loses* precision and the aura of destiny.

5.   You Must Bless The Lord *At All Times*. How nice it would be if you could simply "segment a part of the day" and give Him total focus, and then move on with your tasks. Yet, there is something about the currents of this life...*the whirlpool of busyness*. Satan will not let you have a special time to "get alone with God" without a fight.

Nobody else around you will permit it either.

The very ways of this world keep you sucked in, emptied out, and with no time to just focus on Him and His presence.

Here is your solution. *Bless the Lord at all times.*

Every moment. Each hour. Every day. Make the precious Holy Spirit your total focus and obsession. Others will simply get the *overflow* of His flowing in your life.

At all times. When you are looking at contracts to sign from a realtor, whisper His name. Say quietly, "I love You, precious Holy Spirit." Pray in tongues over and over continuously. "But ye beloved, building up yourselves...praying in the Holy Ghost," (Jude 1:20).

At all times. When I am shaving and trying to get things together in the morning to go to the office, I do not wait until I get into my private place of prayer. Bless Him *at all times*.

You see, when your own dreams and goals become your focus, agitation will erupt. When you are thwarted, someone slows you down or does not follow an instruction, you may become disoriented.

When *others* become your focus, you may become sickened inside when their words wound you. Their countenance may show disdain and contempt for you. Your own family may appear to have been "disappointed in you" because you failed to fulfill their unspoken expectations of you.

The precious Holy Spirit must become your total focus.

My Minister Friend, you cannot "leave" the road and go down a winding path to accommodate every emotional scar and emptiness of your people.

You must *stay with God.*

When you stay with God, *The Hungry for God will find you also.*

When you stay with God, *The Thirsty will observe you and fellowship will begin.*

Bless the Lord at all times.

Become A Worshiper...Yourself.

It is One of the Secrets of the Uncommon Minister.

RECOMMENDED INVESTMENTS:
The Holy Spirit Handbook (Book/B-100/153 Pages/$15)
Where Miracles Are Born (Book/B-115/32 Pages/$7)
The Greatest Day of My Life (Book/B-116/32 Pages/$7)
The Holy Spirit Handbook (6 Tapes/TS-29/$30)

The Opposite Of Truth
Is Confusion.

-MIKE MURDOCK

～ 44 ～

BE WILLING TO PREACH TRUTHS THAT MAY ANGER OTHERS

Truth Always Infuriates Somebody.

The preaching of Jeremiah angered people. "Now Pashur the son of Immer the priest, who was also chief governor in the house of the Lord, heard that Jeremiah prophesied these things. Then Pashur smote Jeremiah the prophet, and put him in the stocks that were in the high gate of Benjamin, which was by the house of the Lord," (Jeremiah 20:1-2).

Here is a remarkable photograph of a preacher's son hating the words of a man of God. His own father was a priest, but he despised the Gospel he heard from *another* minister.

Men of God obey God. Whatever the cost.

The messenger does not always carry *encouraging news*. Many years ago, a preacher declared, "If a man is a true prophet of God, it will be good news and edifying to you." *Wrong.*

True prophets often carry *tragic news*. Jeremiah is an example. "And thou, Pashur, and all that dwell in thine house shall go into captivity: and thou shalt come to Babylon, and there thou shalt die, and shalt be buried there, thou, and all thy friends, to whom thou hast prophesied lies," (Jeremiah 20:6).

6 Facts Every Minister Should Remember About Preaching

1. Preaching Often Intimidates Those With Wrong Motives. Be willing to do as Jesus did: expose the hypocrisy of Pharisees around you. "Woe unto you, scribes and Pharisees, hypocrites! for ye are like unto whited sepulchres, which indeed appear beautiful outward, but are within full of dead men's bones, and of all uncleanness," (Matthew 23:27).

2.   **Preach The Return Of Jesus.** Do it even when millions say that He has delayed His coming. "And saying, Where is the promise of His coming? for since the fathers fell asleep, all things continue as they were from the beginning of the creation," (2 Peter 3:4).

3.   **Preach The Healing Power Of Jesus.** Do it even when some teach erroneously that God is using sickness and disease to correct you. "But He was wounded for our transgressions, He was bruised for our iniquities: the chastisement of our peace was upon Him; and with His stripes we are healed," (Isaiah 53:5).

4.   **Preach The Miracle Power Of God.** Do it even when others say, "That was for the early disciples only." "And God hath set some in the church, first apostles, secondarily prophets, thirdly teachers, after that miracles, then gifts of healings," (1 Corinthians 12:28). "And my speech and my preaching was not with enticing words of man's wisdom, but in demonstration of the Spirit and of power," (1 Corinthians 2:4).

5.   **Preach The Word.** Do it even when others seem to have more fascinating experiences and testimonies. "The prophet that hath a dream, let him tell a dream; and he that hath My Word, let him speak My Word faithfully. What is the chaff to the wheat? saith the Lord. Is not My Word like as a fire? saith the Lord; and like a hammer that breaketh the rock in pieces?" (Jeremiah 23:28-29).

6.   **Preach To Expose False Prophets.** Do it regardless of how clever, cunning and intellectual they appear to be. Jeremiah did. "I have not sent these prophets, yet they ran: I have not spoken to them, yet they prophesied. But if they had stood in My counsel, and had caused My people to hear My words, then they should have turned them from their evil way, and from the evil of their doings," (Jeremiah 23:21-22).

Be Willing To Preach Truths That May Anger Others.
It is One of the Secrets of the Uncommon Minister.

❧ 45 ❧

KNOW YOUR MATE

Your Mate Is Affecting You.
Your mate is affecting your ministry.
Your mate is affecting your people.
Your mate grows your weakness or your strength.
Your mate multiplies your agitation or your peace.

Your mate is helping create the climate of torture or triumph at your house. "Two are better than one; because they have a good reward for their labour," (Ecclesiastes 4:9).

You must invest the time to understand and know your mate if you want to maximize your life and ministry.

5 Facts Ministers Should Know About Their Mates

1. **Know The Wounds Of Your Mate.** A pastor sat in my home weeping. "My wife has not touched me in six months," he wept. "Mike, I cannot take it much longer. I want to be held, touched and loved."

A childhood experience of molestation is a powerful influence that often goes undetected while destroying many marriages.

2. **Know The Fears Of Your Mate.** A young wife tearfully admitted that her father's infidelity and unfaithfulness to her mother had left her embittered. She falsely accused her husband when any behavior reminded her of her father.

3. **Know The Closest Friends Of Your Mate.** Your children are always affected by their friendships at school. They react differently to you after they have been with their friends. Your mate will, also.

"I would not put up with that from my husband," a friend told a pastor's wife. She returned home with volcanic anger. Her friend had only heard one side of the argument. Yet, she embraced the counsel of that uninformed friend.

4. Know Those Who Counsel Your Mate. Never, never, never again will I permit someone I love to receive counsel without me being present. I was shocked and horrified to hear the counsel received by someone I loved several years ago. *Do not send your mate or children to a counselor you do not know well.* In fact, I would urge you to sit in on every counseling session to protect those you love from unwise and distorted counsel.

5. Know The Weaknesses Of Your Mate. Lust? Lying? Imagination? Jealousy? Inferiority? Prevention is often possible when you understand the flaws and weaknesses of your mate. You can protect and build a wall around them.

Know Your Mate.

It is One of the Secrets of the Uncommon Minister.

～ 46 ～

ALWAYS EXIT RELATIONSHIPS GRACIOUSLY

Few Relationships Last Forever.

Even so, it is important to exit every Door of Friendship properly. You cannot enter the next season of your life with joy unless you exit your present season *correctly*.

Recognize when a relationship is ending. Permit it to close with grace and dignity.

Jesus *finished* His work on earth. He cried out from the cross, "It is finished," (John 19:30). Salvation was complete. Redemption had taken place. He had paid the price for the sins of man. Three days later, the resurrection would occur. He would return to the Father where He would make intercession for you and me. He finished *properly*—with the approval of the Father.

Solomon *finished* the Temple. It was an incredible feat. Some have valued the temple today at over 500 billion dollars. Solomon was respected, pursued and celebrated. He *completed* what he started.

Paul *finished* his course. He declared that he had fought a good fight, kept the faith and finished his course. (See 2 Timothy 4:7.) He was a success in the eyes of God. He made his exit from earthly ministry with grace, dignity and passion.

Your ministry will be a collection of *Beginnings*.

Your ministry will also be a collection of *Exits*.

You may not stay in your present church or position forever. You will likely leave your present position. George Barna says the average tenure for a pastor today is 21 months.

8 Ways To Exit Relationships Scripturally

1. **Close Every Door Gently.** Do not slam Doors. Do not

kick Doors. Do not yell at Doors. They are Doors *through which you may want to return again* in the future days of your ministry. Your attitude during *your exit* often determines whether you will ever walk back through the Door again.

    2.   **Close Every Door With Forgiveness.** Unforgiveness is poisonous. It is the cancer that will destroy you from within. Release others to God. Permit Him to do the penalizing or correcting. Like Joseph, recognize that the ultimate plan of God will bring your promotion. "And we know that all things work together for good to them that love God, to them who are the called according to His purpose," (Romans 8:28).

    3.   **Close Every Door With Kindness.** If a church member leaves with cutting and bitter words, refuse to become bitter. "Let all bitterness, and wrath, and anger, and clamour, and evil speaking, be put away from you, with all malice: And be ye kind one to another, tenderhearted, forgiving one another, even as God for Christ's sake hath forgiven you," (Ephesians 4:31-32).

    4.   **Close Every Door With Your Promises Fulfilled.** Finish *what you promise.* Complete your vows. *Whatever* the cost. I test the integrity of others by simply asking myself, "Did he do what he said he would do?" "When thou vowest a vow unto God, defer not to pay it; for He hath no pleasure in fools: pay that which thou hast vowed. Better is it that thou shouldest not vow, than that thou shouldest vow and not pay," (Ecclesiastes 5:4-5).

    The Law of Completed Vows can bring you much peace. Sometimes, people can lose you in the Forest of Words. When they have left, questions can leave you baffled, confused and puzzled. Yet, it is simple. Apply the Law of Completed Vows. Forget the blaming, complaining and accusations. This Law reveals everything you need to know about another person.

    5.   **Close Every Door With Integrity.** Few will do it. People are rarely angry for the reason they tell you. Employees rarely leave for the reason they explain. Much is never discussed. Deception is deadly. It begins when you deceive *yourself.* Then, those around you. Always be honest to others about *the reason* for the Doors closing. It is unnecessary to provide *every* detail. However, it is important that the details you offer are *truthful.*

    6.   **Close Every Door With Courage.** It is not always easy

to close a Door. Sometimes, when you have been involved in a special friendship, it has brought comfort. It has stopped loneliness. It has relieved the burden of emptiness. So, closing a Door requires courage to face the future without that person. Remember who your true *Source* is for every gift you need. Your *Source* is not another person. It is The Holy Spirit, the gift of the Father to you.

He *opens* Doors.

He *closes* Doors.

7. Close Every Door With Expectation Of Supernatural Promotion. The Law of Increase indicates tomorrow is a promotion. God uses the opposite principle of satan. The kingdom of hell operates on the Law of the Sweet and Bitter. Satan offers you the sweet to seduce you. Then, the bitterness destroys. Delilah offered the fragrance of seduction, leaving Samson as the blinded, laughing stock of the Philistines.

God operates in the Law of the Bitter-Sweet. God offers you the bitter first. Then, rewards you with the sweet. Jesus invited us to "take up your cross and follow Me," (Matthew 16:24). Then, the promise was quite clear: if you suffer with Him, you will reign with Him.

Job experienced the Law of the Bitter-Sweet. He went through the bitter season but came out with double blessings. "And the Lord turned the captivity of Job, when he prayed for his friends: also the Lord gave Job twice as much as he had before," (Job 42:10).

When you close Doors gently, you can *expect favor to flow again.* It happened to Job. "Then came there unto him all his brethren, and all his sisters, and all they that had been of his acquaintance before, and did eat bread with him in his house: and they bemoaned him, and comforted him over all the evil that the Lord had brought upon him: every man also gave him a piece of money, and every one an earring of gold," (Job 42:11).

When you close Doors gently, *expect financial multiplication.* It happened to Job. "So the Lord blessed the latter end of Job more than his beginning: for he had fourteen thousand sheep, and six thousand camels, and a thousand yoke of oxen, and a thousand she asses," (Job 42:12).

8. Close Every Door At The Proper Time. Do not close it in a fit of anger. Do not close the Door because of a misunderstanding that erupts. Do not close it because someone *recommends* that you exit. Close the Door in the *Timing of The Holy Spirit.* "To everything there is a season, and a time to every purpose under the heaven...a time to get, and a time to lose; a time to keep, and a time to cast away:..a time to keep silence and a time to speak," (Ecclesiastes 3:1-7).

God Always Brings You Out Of A Place To Bring You Into Another Place. A young man sat in my kitchen a few weeks ago. I was quite concerned. He wanted a position in my ministry. I asked him about his relationship with his previous boss, my pastor friend. He avoided the issue continuously. In fact, I had to ask him the question four or five times before, I received a partial answer. At the end of the conversation, he explained his financial dilemma. He had left a job before ever securing another one. I explained to him how foolish this was. If God were moving him, He would tell him the place where he was to go.

When God told Elijah to leave the brook, Zarephath was scheduled. (Read 1 Kings 17.)

When the Israelites left Egypt, Canaan was the determined destination. (See Exodus 13.)

So, close every Door with God's timing. When you close Doors gently, news will travel...*Good news.*

Always Exit Relationships Graciously.

It is One of the Secrets of the Uncommon Minister.

RECOMMENDED INVESTMENT:
Seeds of Wisdom on Relationships, Volume 2 (Book/B-14/32 Pages/$3)

∼ 47 ∼

HABITUALIZE ORDER AND EXCELLENCE IN ORGANIZING YOUR ENVIRONMENT

Order Is The Accurate Arrangement Of Things.

Order is placing an item where it belongs. Order is keeping your shirts, ties and shoes in the appropriate place in your closet.

Each small act of your life increases *order* or *disorder* around you.

The Purpose Of Order Is To Increase Beauty, *Productivity* And Create *Comfort*. When you walk into a room of order, you want to *stay*. Things are "right." You feel clean, energized and happy. When you walk into a room of clutter and disorder, an unexplainable agitation begins. Sometimes, you are unable to even name it or understand it. Yet, *you were created for order,* and anything that slows you down emotionally or mentally will become a distraction.

When You Increase Order In Your Ministry, You Will Increase Your *Productivity*. Filing cabinets, trays on the desk, and special places for folders make it easier to get your tasks done *on time*. Have you ever shuffled paper after paper in search of a bill? Of course! When you finally located the bill, you were agitated and angry. It affected your entire day. *Disorder influences your attitude* more than you could ever imagine.

***Everything You Are Doing* Is Affecting Order In Your Life.** Think for a moment. You get up from your breakfast table. Either you will leave your plate on the table, or you will take it to the sink. The decision you make will either increase the order or disorder around you. (Leaving it on the table increases your work load and creates disorder. Taking it to the sink *immediately* brings *order*.)

It happened last night for me. I took off my suit coat and laid it over the chair. I did not really feel like taking it over to the closet and hanging it up. Even so, realizing that I was going to hang it up sooner or later, I walked over to the closet and hung up my coat. I immediately increased order around me.

Every Person **Around You Is Increasing Order Or Disorder.** Some people have an *attitude* of disorder. They are unhappy unless everything is in disarray and cluttered. Others refuse to work in such an environment. Their productivity requires organization.

Somebody has said that the arrangement of things in your garage reveals much about your mind. Somebody asked me once, "Does this mean if I do not have a garage, that I really do not have a mind either?" (Smile!) I certainly hope that is not the case, but I am certain psychologists have come to some pretty accurate conclusions.

Every Moment **You Are Increasing Order Or Creating Disorder Around Your Ministry.** Small, tiny actions can eventually produce chaotic situations.

Why do we permit disorder?

Many of us were raised with those who are disorganized. Large families, busy lifestyles or small, cramped apartments can contribute to your attitude.

Some have unusual creativity and simply are uninterested in keeping order around them.

Busyness, moving from place to place, keeps you disorganized. Your mind is on *where you are going* rather than *where you are presently.*

6 Helpful Hints On Order

1. **Recognize The Long-Term Chaos And Losses That Disorder Will Create.** If disorder continues, your momentum will eventually destroy you and your productivity. Successes will become fewer.

2. **Take An Honest And Serious Look At Your Personality.** What can you do to take steps toward change?

3. **Ask Others Who Are Gifted In Organization To Assist You And Keep You On Course.** I read where Donald Trump said that he hired one woman whose entire job was to keep things in order around him.

4. **Do Not Berate Yourself And Become Overly Critical Because Of Your Lack Of Knowledge, Giftings Or Ability To Keep Things In Order.**

5. **Recognize Those Whom God Puts Close To You Who Can Correct Things Around You And Keep Things In Order.**

6. **Do Not Try To Justify Disorder Around You.** Relax, and take a small step today toward order.

It is commendable that you are planning to take an entire week of your vacation to put everything in order in your house next summer. However, I suggest you begin *this very moment* taking some steps to put things in place in the room where you are presently.

Twenty minutes can make a major difference. *Little Hinges Swing Big Doors.* You can get anywhere you want to go if you are willing to take enough small steps.

Develop The Daily Habit Of Order.

It is One of the Secrets of the Uncommon Minister.

RECOMMENDED INVESTMENT:
The School of Wisdom #5: The Law of Order (6 Tapes/TS-45/$30)

Any Movement
Towards Order
Creates Pleasure.

-MIKE MURDOCK

～ 48 ～

ALWAYS KEEP A SMALL DIGITAL RECORDER IN YOUR HAND

Talking Is Faster Than Writing.

Someone has said that you can talk six times faster than you write. I *always* keep note paper and pen handy. *Always.*

However, it is far easier and more productive to dictate in a small digital recorder than it is to write longhand on my legal pad. Admittedly, some of my notes excite me more when I can see them written large in my own handwriting while using a black Sharpie pen. Yet, when there is a flood of ideas and thoughts pouring through me, I consider the small tape recorder to be a gift from God for every achiever.

I have only known two friends in my entire life who keep a digital or tape recorder with them at all times. Others claim to have them "somewhere in their office," or somewhere "down in their briefcase." However, they are not accustomed to using a recorder on a daily basis.

4 Things To Remember About Keeping Your Recorder With You

1. Recording Frees Your Mind From The Stress Of Memory. When you want to remember something, you will often find yourself continuously playing it over and over in your mind...hoping you will not forget it. Consequently, your mind cannot be free for great *ideas,* a season of unusual creativity, or be used in immediate conversations with total focus. Why? Subconsciously, you are trying to *remember* something...to do later or to tell someone.

People try to remember everything. We keep lists, tie strings around our fingers or picture something we want to remember.

I began to produce ten times more with my life when I created the *habit* of keeping a microcassette recorder with me...*every moment of my life.*

2.   Develop The Habit Of Keeping A Recorder Conveniently Close.

At first, it may be uncomfortable. When I started keeping my digital recorder in my pocket, it seemed a little odd, awkward and even cumbersome. After I saw the many pages of material that I produced because of it, it became a joy. It was a constant reminder that great thoughts and ideas flowed through me.

3.   Do Not Feel Obligated To Constantly Record.

There have been times, I have had my microcassette recorder with me for two days and never used it once. Activity around me was so hectic and my schedule so full, everything else required too much from me. Yet, it was *accessible*...handy...convenient. If I did require it, it was there. I was forming the *habit* of dictating.

4.   Making Each Moment Produce Is One Of The Greatest Secrets Of An Uncommon Ministry. Thousands keep waiting for that "perfect time" that they are going to take off a few days or weeks to produce a book, plan a project or design their house.

A decade can pass without any of it occurring, unless you understand how to *turn each moment into a miracle.*

Always Keep A Small Tape Recorder In Your Hand.

It is One of the Secrets of the Uncommon Minister.

RECOMMENDED INVESTMENT:
The School of Wisdom #3: What I'd Do Differently If I Could Start My
   Life Over Again (6 Tapes/TS-43/$30)

～ 49 ～

NEVER REBEL AGAINST A FINANCIAL DELIVERER GOD SENDS TO YOU AND YOUR PEOPLE

Your Ministry Has Not Been Forgotten By God.

Nobody loves you more than the Person who created you. Your fears are *known* by Him. Your tears *matter* to Him.

Your Financial World Matters To God.

12 Facts You Should Remember About Financial Deliverers

1.   When Your Ministry Is Hurting Financially, God Will Bring A Financial Deliverer Toward You. Every moment of your life, God is scheduling miracles. Like currents of blessing, they flow *into* your life and *through* your ministry.

Your prison will have a *door.*

Your river will have a *bridge.*

Your mountain will have a *tunnel.*

Yet, you must find it. Look for it. Listen for it. Search for it. Believe that it exists. "There hath no temptation taken you but such as is common to man: but God is faithful, who will not suffer you to be tempted above that ye are able; but will with the temptation also make a way to escape, that ye may be able to bear it," (1 Corinthians 10:13).

2.   You Must Pursue Those God Is Using To Fuel Your Financial Faith. There are wonderful men and women of God who carry *financial* anointings. They can unlock your faith. It may involve a four-hour drive to their crusade. *It is important that you honor, treasure and pursue that Mantle.* Listen to their tapes. Read their books. Listen to their heart.

They have tasted failure.

They know how to get out of trouble.

They know what sleepless nights are like.

They have defeated the demons of fear.

That is why they are qualified to mentor you and your people.

Some ministers will never taste their Financial Harvest because they are sitting under leaders who fuel their doubts and unbelief. They listen to *church members* who continuously discuss the economic problems on the earth, hard times and how difficult life is.

► *The Voice You Keep Hearing Is The Voice You Will Believe.*

► *The Voice Your People Keep Hearing Is The Voice They Will Believe.*

Ten spies infected millions of Israelites with their unbelief and doubt. When they talked about the giants, the people forgot about the Grapes of Blessing.

What you *talk* about increases.

What you *think* about becomes larger.

Your *mind* and your *mouth* are *magnifiers* of anything you want to grow.

Two spies came back from Canaan with faith, victory and the ability to overcome giants. Their names were Joshua and Caleb. They had been with God.

They had seen the giants, but were not afraid.

They had seen the grapes and decided to become champions. They had experienced too many days in the wilderness to be satisfied with failure. (Read Numbers 13:30-33, 14:1-9.)

They became Champions of Faith. Joshua became the leader of Israel after the death of Moses. Caleb became known for "taking his mountain." Oh, the rewards of faith are so sweet! The taste of victory stays in your mouth so long!

You must discern the Joshuas and Calebs around you. Find faith food. Listen for faith-talk. Sit under it. Listen and absorb.

Something within you will grow. Something within your people will grow.

I receive much inspiration from the story of Elijah and the widow in 1 Kings 17. I never tire of this incredible Well of Wisdom.

She was hurting...devastated...starving. She was one meal from death.

That is when a Financial Deliverer was sent into her life.

He did not criticize her.

He did not coddle her.

He did not sympathize with her.

He knew *how* to get her *out of trouble.*

She had to *listen* to him.

She had to *discern* that he was a man of God.

She had to be *willing* to follow his instructions, regardless of how ridiculous and illogical they seemed to her natural mind.

3.   Another Man Of God Often Holds The Golden Key To Your Financial Deliverance. Can you discern him? If you respect his anointing, chains will fall off. Blindness will disappear. Your eyes will behold the Golden Path to blessing.

If you become critical, resentful and rebellious, you will abort the most remarkable Season of Miracles God has ever scheduled into your life.

Nobody else can *discern* this man of God for you. You must do it yourself.

Nobody else can force you to *obey* this man of God. Your heart must be soft and broken enough to follow God.

4.   You May Receive Only One Opportunity To Obey The Instruction Of A Financial Deliverer That Brings Your Breakthrough. Remember Nabal only received one opportunity to feed and bless the army of David. (Read 1 Samuel 25:2-38.)

5.   You Must Recognize Greatness When You Are In The Presence Of It. It will not always demand attention. Jesus was many places where He was undiscerned, undetected and unrecognized. His own family did not perceive His mantle or His Assignment. "For neither did His brethren believe in Him," (John 7:5).

6.   You May Have To Seek Out The Man Of God Before He Pursues You. You see, he is not really needing you. You need him.

Read the incredible story of Saul and his servant, who had lost their donkeys. They were so disturbed *until the servant remembered that a man of God lived in the area.* The servant knew the power of giving an offering. They made the decision to find the Prophet Samuel. The rest of the story is absolutely remarkable. When they came into the presence of Samuel, the anointing of the prophet began to flow toward Saul.

They *sowed* an offering.

They *believed* a man of God.

That encounter with Samuel catapulted Saul into the kingship of Israel. (Read 1 Samuel 9-11.)

7.   Somewhere, There Is A Man Of God With The Golden Key To Your Door Of Blessing. Your responsibility is to *find* him, *discern* him and *obey* his instructions.

Several years ago, my assistant listened to me share the miracle of the "Covenant of Blessing," the sowing of the $58 Seed.

My first encounter was in Washington, DC, when The Holy Spirit instructed me to plant a Seed of $58 to represent the 58 kinds of blessings I had found in Scripture. My obedience launched an incredible parade of miracles into my personal life and ministry. I have told about this everywhere.

My assistant was a fine young man who loved God. Faith came alive as he listened to me tell my experience. I instructed him and others present in that service to give their Seed "an Assignment."

"Write on your check where you need the Harvest in your own life," I instructed.

He planted his Seed of $58, and wrote "better family relations" on his check. Seven amazing miracles happened following his Seed of Obedience.

▶   His mother accepted Christ within 14 days.

▶   His two sisters accepted Christ within 14 days.

▶   His daughter accepted Christ within 14 days.

▶   He was able to spend a week with two of his daughters he had not seen in five years.

▶ He was able to have a meal with his entire family, which had not happened in fifteen years.

▶ His eighty-six year old father accepted Christ within ninety days.

▶ His oldest sister, who had run away from home forty-eight years earlier, was found!

She came back home for a family reunion.

Nobody had seen or heard from her for those forty-eight long years. She had been thought to be dead.

Every one of these miracles happened within ninety days of his sowing his Seed of $58.

He had simply followed the instruction of a man of God.

Almost everywhere I go, I ask those who need miracles to plant a Seed...*a specific Seed.* Often, I invite believers to plant a Seed of $58. Sometimes, it is more, depending on the leading of God in the services. The miracles are incredible. I get letters from everywhere relating the supernatural intervention of God *following their acts of obedience.*

A woman in Knoxville, Tennessee, approached me with a tall husband by her side. "Remember that Seed of $58?" she asked.

"Yes."

"This is him!" He had been away from Christ. Within a few days after her Seed, he came to church with her and gave his heart to God!

8. The Financial Deliverer God Sends To You May Not Be Packaged As You Desire. John the Baptist had an appearance many could not tolerate. Yet, God was with him. *God's greatest gifts do not always arrive in silk.* He often uses burlap bags to package His best prizes. "The Lord seeth not as man seeth; for man looketh on the outward appearance, but the Lord looketh on the heart," (1 Samuel 16:7).

9. The Financial Deliverer God Sends Into Your Church May Have An Abrasive Or Uncomfortable Personality. If you could have heard Isaiah or Ezekiel, you might be shocked at some of the strong language that poured from their lips.

10. The Financial Deliverer God Sends With A Special

Challenge To Your Church May Even Be A Social Misfit. God often uses foolish things to confound the wise. You will not discern them through the hearing of the ear nor the seeing of the eye. "But God hath chosen the foolish things of the world to confound the wise; and God hath chosen the weak things of the world to confound the things which are mighty," (1 Corinthians 1:27).

11. You Will Only Discern Your Financial Deliverer By The Spirit Of God Within You. "Believe in the Lord your God, so shall ye be established; believe His prophets, so shall ye prosper," (2 Chronicles 20:20).

12. When You Begin To Acknowledge The Word Of The Lord Coming From Proven And Established Servants Of God, The Flow Of Miracles Will Multiply And Increase Toward You And Your People.

Never Rebel Against A Financial Deliverer God Sends To You And Your People.

It is One of the Secrets of the Uncommon Minister.

RECOMMENDED INVESTMENTS:
31 Reasons People Do Not Receive Their Financial Harvest (Book/B-82/ 252 Pages/$12)
7 Keys To 1000 Times More (Book/B-104/128 Pages/$10)
7 Keys To 1000 Times More (6 Tapes/TS-30/$30)
31 Reasons People Do Not Receive Their Financial Harvest (6 Tapes/ TS-38/$30)

≈ 50 ≈

VALIDATE YOUR MESSAGE WITH SUFFICIENT AND SUPPORTIVE SCRIPTURES

Information Births Confidence.

Several years ago, one of my favorite young preachers stated that he wanted me to "father" him much more.

"I want to be your son in the Lord," he said.

"All right. Can you handle correction? Because that is part of the purpose of a father," I explained. He insisted that he could.

"Tonight, you spoke and preached for one hour and forty minutes. You quoted less than four Scriptures in almost two hours of preaching. Son, I speak to you as your spiritual father—*you do not know The Word of God.* It shows. You tell Bible stories but, provide no Scriptural reference. No memorization has obviously occurred in your life. The Bible is a sermon book to you. It is a starting point for your spiritual arguments. However, as your spiritual father, I am compelled to tell you that you must know The Word of God before you can bring deliverance and healing to those who are in captivity."

He looked at me woodenly. Our relationship became strained from that night. *I was not being critical.* I had the same conversation with a man of God many years ago, at the beginning of my ministry...on the receiving end! *The First Step Toward Success Is The Willingness To Listen.*

5 Keys To Effective Study

1.   Establish A Specific Place For Reading Your Bible. Certainly, you can read it anywhere at any time. Yet, the habit of climate and atmosphere is powerful. Your family should even know when and where they can observe you reading your Bible every day.

2. Keep A Personal Wisdom Journal Of Your Discoveries In The Word Of God. Someone has said, "A short pencil is better than a long memory." Do not try to remember everything you read. Document it. Discuss it. Talk about it to others. *Begin to live* what you read that very day.

3. Expect The Holy Spirit To Illuminate And Magnify The Specific Truth Most Appropriate For Your Present Circumstances. I will never forget September 24, 1997. Why? That is the day when The Holy Spirit magnified the topic, "The Mantle Called Love." He showed me the importance of living by Love, speaking in Love, and walking in Love toward others. Everything that day was magnified...in the light of Love. Every day will be different. Expect The Holy Spirit to teach you Uncommon Wisdom during uncommon moments with His Word.

4. Teach Your People What You Are Learning In The Word. I believe in 31 day and 365 day teaching programs that take you through the entire Word of God. However, the most exciting days of my ministry have occurred when I spoke spontaneously and extemporaneously on the topic that had excited my heart *that very morning during prayer.* Sometimes, I wanted to delay speaking on it until I did more research. Yet, I have learned that when The Holy Spirit excites your heart, that is the focus He wants you to move toward that very day.

5. Determine To Become An Expert On One Topic In Scripture. At the present, I am currently laboring to memorize 365 Scriptures concerning The Word of God. Why? I am persuaded that The Word of God is the most important force in a person's life.

▶ It is the Key to *Change.*

▶ It is the Key to *Joy.*

▶ It is the Key to *Peace.*

▶ It is the *Master Key To Life*—The Word of God.

Perhaps, you are led by The Spirit to study healing, salvation or love. Whatever topic you choose, develop a calendar of 365 verses and purpose to become a scriptural authority on that one topic.

Validate Your Message With Sufficient And Supportive Scriptures.

It is One of the Secrets of the Uncommon Minister.

⇜ 51 ⇝

PROTECT YOUR FOCUS EVERY SINGLE DAY

The Only Reason Men Fail Is Broken Focus.

While traveling around the world for more than 41 years and speaking to more than 16,000 audiences in 40 countries, I have listened to the details of the personal battles and conflicts of many hurting people. As I have listened, I have learned a very important truth: An important goal of satan is to simply break the focus of God's people from their Assignments. *Focus is anything that consumes your time, energy, finances and attention.* So if satan can blur the focus of your Assignment, he can master you. If he can master you, he can bring pain to the heart of God...Who is his only true enemy.

How important is your focus?

Listen to the words of God concerning those who would tempt His people to go to another god:

"If thy brother, the son of thy mother, or thy son, or thy daughter, or the wife of thy bosom, or thy friend, which is as thine own soul, entice thee secretly, saying, Let us go and serve other gods, which thou hast not known, thou, nor thy fathers; Namely, of the gods of the people which are round about you, nigh unto thee, or far off from thee, from the one end of the earth even unto the other end of the earth; Thou shalt not consent unto him, nor hearken unto him; neither shall thine eye pity him, neither shalt thou spare, neither shalt thou conceal him: But thou shalt surely kill him; thine hand shall be first upon him to put him to death, and afterwards the hand of all the people. And thou shalt stone him with stones, that he die; because he hath sought to thrust thee away from the Lord thy God, which brought thee out of the land of Egypt, from the house of bondage," (Deuteronomy 13:6-10).

Now listen to how *Jesus* addressed *broken focus* in the New Testament:

"And if thy right eye offend thee, pluck it out, and cast it from thee: for it is profitable for thee that one of thy members should perish, and not that thy whole body should be cast into hell. And if thy right hand offend thee, cut it off, and cast it from thee: for it is profitable for thee that one of thy members should perish, and not that thy whole body should be cast into hell," (Matthew 5:29-30).

***Jesus* Encouraged *His Disciples* To Keep *Their Focus* On The Kingdom Of God.** He assured them that their financial provisions and everything they needed would be produced through absolute focus upon Him:

"But seek ye first the kingdom of God, and His righteousness; and all these things shall be added unto you," (Matthew 6:33).

How do you destroy someone's goal? Give him another goal. How do you destroy another's dream? You give him another dream. Why? *It fragments his focus.* It dilutes his energy. So to avoid this in your Assignment, here are twelve Wisdom Principles on Focus that can make a real difference in your life.

12 Wisdom Principles On Focus

1. **Focus Determines Mastery.** Anything that has the ability to *keep* your attention has mastered you. So, any significant progress toward the completion of your Assignment will require every thought, cent and hour of your life.

2. **Your Focus Determines Your Energy.** Think for a moment. Let's say you are sleepy, laid back on your pillows, and the television is on. Then suddenly, the telephone rings. Someone in your family has just had a crisis and they are being rushed to the hospital. Do you go back to sleep? Of course not. Your focus has been changed. Suddenly, you have leapt to your feet, put your clothes on, jumped in your car and are headed to the hospital. Your new focus gave you new energy. It determined your energy.

3. **What You Look At The Longest Becomes The Strongest In Your Life.** The apostle Paul focused on his future: "Brethren, I count not myself to have apprehended: but this one thing I do, forgetting those things which are behind, and reaching forth unto those things which are before, I press toward the mark for the prize of the high calling of God in Christ Jesus," (Philippians 3:13-14).

4. Broken Focus Creates Insecurity And Instability In Everything Around You. "A double minded man is unstable in all his ways," (James 1:8).

5. Only Focused Faith Can Produce Miracles From The Hand Of God. "But let him ask in faith, nothing wavering. For he that wavereth is like a wave of the sea driven with the wind and tossed. For let not that man think that he shall receive any thing of the Lord," (James 1:6-7).

6. Sight Affects Desire. What you keep looking upon, you will eventually pursue.

"Mine eye affecteth mine heart," (Lamentations 3:51).

Joshua, the remarkable leader of the Israelites, wrote this instruction from God:

"Only be thou strong and very courageous, that thou mayest observe to do according to all the law, which Moses My servant commanded thee: turn not from it to the right hand or to the left, that thou mayest prosper whithersoever thou goest. This book of the law shall not depart out of thy mouth; but thou shalt meditate therein day and night, that thou mayest observe to do according to all that is written therein: for then thou shalt make thy way prosperous, and then thou shalt have good success," (Joshua 1:7-8).

7. Focusing On The Word Of God Daily Is Necessary To Complete Your Assignment Properly. God instructed the people of Israel to teach, train and mentor their children. Why? *His Words.* Listen to this incredible instruction:

"Therefore shall ye lay up these My words in your heart and in your soul, and bind them for a sign upon your hand, that they may be as frontlets between your eyes. And ye shall teach them your children, speaking of them when thou sittest in thine house, and when thou walkest by the way, when thou liest down, and when thou risest up. And thou shalt write them upon the door posts of thine house, and upon thy gates," (Deuteronomy 11:18-20).

8. Focusing, Hearing And Speaking The Word Of God Continuously Makes You Invincible. This is one of the reasons I keep cassettes of The Word of God in every room of my home. The first thing I do daily is turn on my tape player to listen to the Scriptures being read. It washes my mind, purges my heart and harnesses my focus.

"There shall no man be able to stand before you: for the Lord your God shall lay the fear of you and the dread of you upon all the land that ye shall tread upon, as He hath said unto you," (Deuteronomy 11:25).

9. Focus Has Reward. "That your days may be multiplied, and the days of your children, in the land which the Lord sware unto your fathers to give them, as the days of heaven upon the earth. For if ye shall diligently keep all these commandments which I command you, to do them, to love the Lord your God, to walk in all His ways, and to cleave unto Him; Then will the Lord drive out all these nations from before you, and ye shall possess greater nations and mightier than yourselves. Every place whereon the soles of your feet shall tread shall be yours," (Deuteronomy 11:21-24).

10. What You Keep Seeing Determines Your Focus. "I will set no wicked thing before mine eyes: I hate the work of them that turn aside; it shall not cleave to me," (Psalm 101:3).

11. Your Enemy Is Anyone Who Breaks Your Focus From A God-Given Assignment. "Do thy diligence to come shortly unto me: For Demas hath forsaken me, having loved this present world, and is departed unto Thessalonica; Crescens to Galatia, Titus unto Dalmatia," (2 Timothy 4:9-10).

12. Your Friend Is Anyone Who Helps Keep You Focused On The Instructions Of God For Your Life. "Having confidence in thy obedience I wrote unto thee, knowing that thou wilt also do more than I say," (Philemon 1:21).

6 Keys That Will Help You Protect Your Focus

1. Recognize That Broken Focus Will Destroy Your Dreams. Distraction from your Assignment will create an unending parade of tragedies and disasters in your life.

2. Take Personal Responsibility. Be the gatekeeper of your eyes, ears and heart. Nobody else can fully protect you. You will be protected by God, as you yield yourself to Him.

3. Control The Music And Teaching That Enters Your Ears. *What You Hear Determines What You Feel.* What you hear also determines what you fear.

"And all Israel shall hear, and fear, and shall do no more any such wickedness as this is among you," (Deuteronomy 13:11).

4.   Keep Continuous Praise On Your Lips And Music Throughout Your Home. I keep music playing twenty-four hours a day on my property and in my house. The rooms throughout my home have sound, and there is music to The Holy Spirit being sung and played every minute. I have twenty-four speakers on the trees in my seven-acre yard. I am determined to protect my focus.

5.   Starve Wrong Friendships. Wrong friends do not feed, fuel or fertilize the total focus of your Assignment. So let those friendships die. Samson did not have to date everyone to get his haircut. It only required *one* wrong person to destroy his future. Permit Distractions To Die...

6.   Pursue And Permit Only Those Relationships That Increase Your Focus On Your Assignment. It was late one night in southern Florida. The service had ended, and several ministers wanted to go to a restaurant. As we sat there, I listened to their conversation. I have two major interests in my life: learning and teaching. Both must take place continuously for me to have pleasure!

So I sat there and listened as everyone discussed ball games, politics and tragedies. I kept listening for worthy Wisdom Keys that might be imparted, and for important questions that might be asked. Neither took place. Several times I even attempted to change the direction of the conversation, but it seemed to be ignored. The Holy Spirit was not the focus, and I was too tired to force the conversation in an appropriate direction. So I quietly stood and said, "I must leave. God bless each of you." Then, I left. I wish I could have that kind of courage every year of my lifetime, every day of my life.

Focus Is The Master Key To The Golden Door Of Success.

Protect Your Focus.

It is One of the Secrets of the Uncommon Minister.

RECOMMENDED INVESTMENTS:
The Leadership Secrets of Jesus (Book/B-91/196 pages/$12)
Secrets of the Richest Man Who Ever Lived (6 Tapes/TS-25/$30)

You Will Only Have
Significant Success
With Something That
Is An Obsession.

-MIKE MURDOCK

～ 52 ～

Create A Training Program On DVD For Your Team And Protégés

Stop Repeating Yourself.
Teach Your Wisdom...via Videos and DVD's.

The Greatest Secret Of My Ministry Staff

Forty years of World Evangelism, creates an ocean of *Experiences, Disappointments and Tragedies.*

Your staff...will control, birth, decide MOST of your emotions, victories, failures, and they will be targeted by "The 3rd Voice" that distracts them...discourages them...destroys them.

Your Voice Matters.

Your Mentorship Matters.

Your Experiences affect your Team, Protégés and Family.

Your Instructions, Experiences and Expectations are the foundation for a decisive, passionate and competent team.

The Disturbing Thought I Had

I came home from a long trip. When I arrived at my office, my leaders were uncomfortable, blabbering and almost absurd. They could not look me in the eye. Their conversations were jerky, unfocused and deceptive.

Within hours, I knew why. None of my instructions via phone had been followed. None of the Team Departments had received my deposits of Mentorship...intended through my Management Team.

I fired the five people most responsible.

I then created a library of 60 DVD's on 60 different topics...such as "How to Answer the Phone," "The Importance of My Partners."

I placed a huge viewing screen on the wall...in a designated "Mentorship Room." I established "Team-Talks"-Mentorship Moments with Mike Murdock.

Note taking is *required, reviewed* and *evaluated.* Mentorship...became habitual.

Expectations are clarified, articulated...*every single day. What You Keep Hearing, You Will Eventually Understand.*

Over 16 hours of DVD Training...is the first priority of anyone hired on the staff. Three videos are required *before* hiring.

Sheep Will Follow The Voice They Hear Most

I do not want anyone else...teaching My Heart to My Team.

Jesus...taught His own disciples.

Jesus...invested time in His own team.

Jesus...was The Voice that silenced the doubts birthed by Pharisees.

Jesus...answered the questions from Peter on the "Reward System." (See Mark 10:28-29.)

My Precious Minister Friend, do not let ANYONE ELSE Mentor your staff.

Judas...left a family. Absalom left a genealogy.

The Traitor and the Disloyal abound.

Silence them through the Repetition...The System of Personal Mentorship.

It Is The Master Secret Of Building A Passionate Loyal Team.

DR. MIKE MURDOCK

1 Has embraced his Assignment to Pursue...Proclaim...and Publish the Wisdom of God to help people achieve their dreams and goals.

2 Preached his first public sermon at the age of 8.

3 Preached his first evangelistic crusade at the age of 15.

4 Began full-time evangelism at the age of 19, which has continued since 1966.

5 Has traveled and spoken to more than 16,000 audiences in 40 countries, including East and West Africa, the Orient, Europe and South America.

6 Noted author of over 200 books, including best sellers, *Wisdom for Winning, Dream Seeds, The Double Diamond Principle, The Law of Recognition* and *The Holy Spirit Handbook.*

7 Created the popular *Topical Bible* series for Businessmen, Mothers, Fathers, Teenagers; *The One-Minute Pocket Bible* series, and *The Uncommon Life* series.

8 The Creator of the Master 7 Mentorship Program, an Achievement Program for Believers.

9 Has composed thousands of songs such as "I Am Blessed," "You Can Make It," "God Rides On Wings Of Love" and "Jesus, Just The Mention Of Your Name," recorded by many gospel artists.

10 Is the Founder and Senior Pastor of The Wisdom Center, in Fort Worth, Texas...a Church with International Ministry around the world.

11 Host of *Wisdom Keys with Mike Murdock,* a weekly TV Program seen internationally.

12 Has appeared often on TBN, CBN, BET, Daystar, Inspirational Network, LeSea Broadcasting and other television network programs.

13 Has led over 3,000 to accept the call into full-time ministry.

192

THE MINISTRY

1 **Wisdom Books & Literature** - Over 200 best-selling Wisdom Books and 70 Teaching Tape Series.

2 **Church Crusades** - Multitudes are ministered to in crusades and seminars throughout America in "The Uncommon Wisdom Conferences." Known as a man who loves pastors, he has focused on church crusades for over 41 years.

3 **Music Ministry** - Millions have been blessed by the anointed songwriting and singing of Mike Murdock, who has made over 15 music albums and CDs available.

4 **Television** - *Wisdom Keys with Mike Murdock,* a nationally-syndicated weekly television program.

5 **The Wisdom Center** - The Church and Ministry Offices where Dr. Murdock speaks weekly on Wisdom for The Uncommon Life.

6 **Schools of The Holy Spirit** - Mike Murdock hosts Schools of The Holy Spirit in many churches to mentor believers on the Person and Companionship of The Holy Spirit.

7 **Schools of Wisdom** - In many major cities Mike Murdock hosts Schools of Wisdom for those who want personalized and advanced training for achieving "The Uncommon Dream."

8 **Missions Outreach** - Dr. Mike Murdock's overseas outreaches to 40 countries have included crusades in East and West Africa, the Orient, Europe and South America.